Along Featherbed Lane

Bromley Stores had been built on the front of 4 Bromley Villas, our new home.

The view from our front bedroom window, over the roof of Bromley Stores. The hedgerow on the far side of the nearby field shows the path taken by the lower part of Featherbed Lane.

Along Featherbed Lane

Christine Beech

Beech Publishing House

Copyright © 2017 by Christine Beech

All rights reserved. This book or any portion thereof may not be reproduced or used in any manner whatsoever without the express written permission of the publisher except for the use of brief quotations in a book review or scholarly journal.

The moral rights of the author have been asserted

First Printing: 2017
Reprinted: 2025

Beech Publishing House

Contents

Prologue: Going home   1
1: A new beginning   3
2: Bromley Stores   6
3: Starting school   12
4: Neighbours   18
5: Cats and kittens   25
6: Ill health   31
7: Managing   40
8: Brothers   49
9: Visiting Grandma   53
10: Mrs Long   60
11: Stormy weather   71
12: Going to church   81
13: Moving on   88
14: Chew Valley School   91
15: A new friend   95
16: Camping   103
17: High days and holidays   112
18: Jennie   119

Prologue: Going home

I always skipped when I was going home. Home was a valley, where the mist lingered in the morning and the afternoon was drowsy with pollen. And I dithered along with the breeze down Featherbed Lane gathering posies of primroses and violets in spring and, as the year matured, blackberries, crab apples and elderberries for jam, jelly and wine.

Autumn came suddenly with the wind at night and in the morning filled the house with the sweetness of fallen apples, bruised and gently rotting in the boxes spread over the kitchen floor. My mother knew that the brown pulp would spread until all must be thrown away and yet, for the polished ripeness of the rest, she kept each one I had picked for her from the mud. Storms tore the fruit from the trees and even uprooted the trees at times but the harvest was carefully tucked away into the oak cabinet brimming with gleaming jars of pickles and jams. Inside the house lapped by wind, all was still.

Late some other summer I returned, walking until the roads dwindled into the lanes of childhood. Hoary with clematis, stooped and muttering as these old hedges were in winter, this summer they spread out their skirts rustling with speckled life. I stopped for a moment, quite still, taut as the rabbit raised on its haunches to twitch the air before hurrying into its burrow. No one was about. The child who used to hide from the tractors in neighbouring fields could go on.

Along Featherbed Lane

The trees had stopped singing of summer and the wind broke over my ears. It had rained that morning. The holly, polished for its season, stood steady above the wisps of grass turned to straw at the roots. Having no basket, I idled the blackberries from twig to mouth. Each sweet berry burst bitter along the tongue. A bee crawled before me along the road. He had flown too far; gathered too little sweetness. Now he floundered on with wings of leaded glass. The primroses were gone and, high above, the foxgloves pouted.

Along the wires swallows fidgeted, interrupted, finished one another's phrase. In a garden the honesty, which had wept away its petals in high summer, was still shedding brown paper to squander its silver to the shredding wind. Wood smoke from an undying country bonfire stung my eyes and for a moment blotted out the house. Then I saw it. I had been told. 'Smoking in bed she'd been,' they said, 'lucky to be alive.' Where the tiles had been cushioned with moss and house martins had nested, there was nothing left. The roof was cracked open like a snail's shell crushed between stone and the thrush's beak.

Chapter 1: A new beginning

Moving to the tiny hamlet of Bromley in the Chew Valley in 1966 was in every sense a new beginning and the fulfilment of my mother's long-held dream to live in the countryside. Born on the 18th December 1960, my previous life in Bristol was for me just a few shafts of memory. For me, life began at the age of five as my family moved into Bromley Stores.

It was a cold, bleak January start. Mum was ill with the quinsy and spent her time in her new, rose-patterned bedroom nursing an injured jackdaw. Much to our neighbours' amusement, Mum always took in any stranded fledglings or cat-mauled birds that came our way. Most closed their eyes on our amateurish attempts to save them after a day or so. Still, a few did survive, to be reunited on a low rooftop with excited parent birds. Memory of such successes strengthened us to cope with the far more frequent loss of a small, fluttering life to twig-like stiffness. However, in this case, both Mum and the jackdaw soon rallied and our daily pattern of life could begin.

None of us were quite prepared for how cold country life was going to be. Downstairs was heated by two coal fires: one in the living room, just behind the shop, and the other in the dining room. Upstairs may have had electric bar fires but I have no memory of anything taking the edge off the bitter chill of those bedrooms. Bedtime involved adding layers of fleecy nightdresses,

Along Featherbed Lane

bedsocks, bedjacket or old cardigan and dressing gown and snuggling up to a hot-water bottle. In the morning the insides of the windows were thickly covered with swirling patterns of ice, which stayed there until the midday sun poured them over the windowsills.

Winds swept savagely across the hilltop fields, having no mercy on our small huddle of houses. If you went outside when the strong winds blew, you took shelter against the high hedgerows and slowly crept your way back to the house in their protection.

Going outdoors was an all-weather necessity, unfortunately, as the only toilet was a few yards away in the back garden, the far side of a public right of way that ran along behind our row of houses. A large privet hedge ran beside the toilet, providing a sheltered pathway for the last few steps. Outside the back door the pitch blackness of the countryside engulfed you. The feeble rays from the torch you carried scarcely penetrated it. The toilet itself was a place of lurking shadows, hung with anaemic spiders crouching in the cobwebs. Where the whitewash had chipped away from the uneven walls, I pictured animals and faces and whiled away my time weaving them into stories.

Creepy and inconvenient it may have been but this toilet also provided us with tales of laughter over the years. My elder brother Jonathan once arrived late in the evening with a friend from Oxford. 'I'm really sorry about this,' he murmured. 'The only toilet's actually outside. Still, it's only a short walk away. Mind you, it

A new beginning

might be worth putting your coat and scarf back on. It gets pretty cold around here at night.' He then proceeded to lead the way there via the garden paths of all our neighbours' open-plan gardens, a detour of at least 450 feet each way!

On another occasion, my Mum was enjoying a good session of nose-blowing in the privacy of the toilet. She did have a remarkably resonant nose, which carried its booming tone quite some distance. On this occasion, Geoff, a local builder and smallholder who lived three doors away, gathered his labourers together to work out where the mysterious sound echoing its way round the hamlet was coming from.

'Must be a buzz saw over at Stanton Wick.'

'Don't be daft, it's one of Farmer Baber's cows got loose. It's probably after the pigswill and all, round the back of yourn!'

By the time they had got to our coal shed, Geoff put his fingers to his lips and ushered his men back to their yard. Red-faced, he doubled over in laughter.

'You daft lot! You've never heard Mrs Longhurst blowing her nose in the outside toilet before, have yer?'

Chapter 2: Bromley Stores

Our home was the left-hand end of a terrace of four small houses. It was much more than this though, for instead of a small patch of front garden, it had a shop attached to its front wall, with our living-room window looking directly into it.

A layer of net curtain gave me what I liked to pretend was the privilege of a one-way view into Dad's world. Customers rarely commented on the goings-on in our home, whether from politeness or from the sheer everyday nature of what they saw.

However, I'll always remember the day when my home-made ginger beer exploded from its bottle, buckling back the lid as I started to unscrew it. Both our newly decorated living room and I were showered in pungent stickiness.

''Ere, Mr Longhurst,' a local lad in the shop shouted out, 'You'd never believe what a mess that daughter of yourn is making.'

'How dare he look into my home and tell tales on me! How dare he!' I muttered savagely at my poor mum. I was so incensed that I completely overlooked the fact that I had wrecked her lovely wallpaper.

Dust crept under the shop door along with the occasional field mouse and swarmed around the glass-fronted cabinets at the stroke of a broom, freckling the sunlit air. Sunshine basked in the window with the twice-turned tins and a spider who, if the curtain twitched, hid

Bromley Stores

under his corner of parched lining paper. A frowzy blowfly, haranguing the air, jousted with the window pane. A fragrance of ripe apples drenched the usual blend of potatoes, green-sprigged tomatoes, tea and tobacco.

I loved the quietness and order that reigned there, under Dad's authority. It was the best place to go for a chat with Dad or just to be together, enjoying the sunny stillness. Dad would sit behind the chocolate display cabinet making a rug across his lap, whilst I sat on the counter, swinging my legs. As far as I was concerned, customers were an intrusion. The spider scuttled for refuge and so did I, unless caught by a greeting.

Dad, however, was a wonderful shopkeeper. He had made his previous shop, White Tree Electrical and Toy Bazaar, into a thriving business. Winning vital agencies from the top toy manufacturers of the day (Lego, Scalextric, Hornby and Meccano) and having a rare gift for making intricate repairs on the model trains and cars helped enormously. Leaving this precious business in the hands of a manager must have been a wrench for Dad but his desire to make Mum happy was an overriding principle for him.

Bromley Stores had also done bustling trade in its earlier days. Our elderly landlady, Mrs Brown, had lost her young husband in the First World War. Her father built the shop on the front of her home as a way of giving her an independent income and a purpose for her life.

In those days there was a coal mine at Bromley and the store soon became the miners' shop, kitting them out

Along Featherbed Lane

with all they needed in the way of mining clothes and equipment as well as providing a general stores for their families.

Now the pit was long closed, leaving behind it a small slag heap, half landscaped with trees. Leaves fossilised in slate had been flung to the surface and gorse bushes held on for dear life. Occasionally an echo from the empty shafts could be felt shuddering under our kitchen floor.

There was still a little local industry. At the foot of the hill was a firm that hired out large agricultural machinery for the use of local farmers. These drivers were our principal customers, coming in early morning on their way to work for bottles of Dandelion & Burdock or Cherryade, cigarettes, bars of chocolate, chunks of Cheddar cheese and packets of crisps. Then, on their way home, the younger ones would pop back for more refreshments and tubs of soothing creams to ease their sun or wind-chapped skin, sold with sympathy by Mum.

Between these two relative rush hours, the shop was often empty. A few locals bought the bulk of their groceries from us but, with two more shops down in the village and supermarkets springing up within driving distance, business was never likely to be brisk. It annoyed Dad immensely that supermarkets sold items far more cheaply than he could buy them from the wholesaler. It also infuriated him when customers boasted to us of their bargains from afar, without a thought of the cost of petrol involved.

Bromley Stores

However, with the profits from our business in Bristol providing our income, the poor trade at Bromley could be overlooked. The shop was treated more like a hobby than a serious business venture. Dad still took in repairs, working late in the corner of the shop and taking pride in his renown for this craftsmanship. Sharing Dad's short-sightedness, I enjoyed watching and learning a little of this fiddly work. I loved helping to wind bright copper wire smoothly onto tiny armatures.

Dad soon picked up the expertise needed for running a general store. Using a length of wire fastened at one end to the marble cheese block and at the other to a wooden handle, he deftly sliced the right weight of cheese off the truckles of Cheddar. For Mum and Dad, the right weight in business was not the exact weight but a little over. The surplus came as a free bonus to make the customer feel that they had received good measure.

Everything was weighed on an old-fashioned balance scales. The purchase was placed in a large brown or small white paper bag and then somersaulted over to twist the top of the bag by way of a seal. On the other side of the scales was a set of weights. Brass nesting ones were used for the ounces and handled lead ones for the pounds. For really large purchases, slabs of lard would be fetched from the fridge to act as counterbalance. Old-fashioned it may have been, yet this set of scales always passed the exacting tests set it by the 'weights and measures' man when he came on his routine spot-check visits.

Along Featherbed Lane

Our till was also very basic, just a long wooden box with a roll of paper showing through a hole in the lid of the box. On this the cost of any purchase was carefully written and the balance totted up at the end of the day. A long drawer at the bottom of the box pulled out to reveal several compartments for coins and notes. Even more intriguing for me as a child was the complex of small square drawers set against the wall behind the counter. Although there must have been twenty-four or more of these identical drawers, Dad easily remembered the contents of each one. I loved testing him and carefully opening each to reveal balls of string, drawing pins, tiny tins of Humbrol paint and so on.

The most modern item of equipment in the shop was our freezer. This stood proudly in the well of the shop next to the display of Jamaican Ginger and Granny cakes, Lyons apple pies and Majorca slices. It was white and the shape of a tea chest, with a pale blue lid. Stock was at the top, mostly choc ices and small rectangles of vanilla ice cream in greaseproof paper to serve between wafers. Chilled Mars Bars were also very popular. Hidden underneath were tubs filled with home-grown fruit, stashed away for the long winter days ahead.

Cigarettes were, to Mum's disgust, our best source of income. Most memorable, however, was Dad's wonderful display of sweets and chocolate. Our pride and joy was the Fry's display cabinet in dark wood with glass panels to reveal the bars of chocolate. A row of large shilling bars of Dairy Milk, Whole Nut and Fruit & Nut

Bromley Stores

was at the front. To the side of them were the ordinary sixpenny and fourpenny bars of Milk Tray, Mars, Crunchie, Aero and Bounty. Underneath were the small Animal Bars, Walnut Whips, Milky Ways, Milky Bars and Chocolate Buttons. Tucked at the back were plain white bags of lucky dip sweets at a penny or tuppence a time. Children spent long, wonderful minutes gazing into that cabinet before making their choice.

Fancy new brands ended up in special display boxes on the counter. Old Jamaica chocolate bars and Raspberry Ripples were particular favourites that kept this pole position for many months. Best of all, though, were the large jars of sweets to be weighed. These were lined up on four wooden shelves behind the counter with eight or so jars per shelf. Sherbet Lemons, liquorice sticks, cough candy, pineapple chunks, Fox's Glacier mints, Nuttall's Mintoes and oh so many others jostled for attention.

Chapter 3: Starting school

It was my brother Patrick who took me to school for the first time, on a bleak day in January. I was appalled at the thought of having so much time away from my family and not impressed to be spending it with other children. I had played a little with the two boys of my age who lived in Bromley. However, my main playmates had always been Jonathan and Patrick, who were seventeen and thirteen years older than me. The oldest boys in the Junior part of the school caught my eye as the most promising candidates for friends, but somehow this never worked out!

Our school nestled quietly up a lane the far side of Stanton Drew. My year was quite a large intake into a school whose numbers had dwindled to a total of less than thirty for Juniors and Infants combined. By the time I left, this total had reached over seventy and the school's future was secured.

My first taste of school was short-lived. My parents had no car and argued that children from our hamlet should be entitled to a school taxi. The authorities disagreed and refused to help. I was withdrawn from school until they changed their minds. The school inspector was sent round to lecture my parents on the harm they were doing to my education. Mum always loved a challenge. She set out to prove her ability as a teacher and mine as a student. She succeeded. Soon after my return to school some weeks later, we were given a

Starting school

reading test. To everyone's amazement, I had a reading age of over eleven years, the second best in the entire school.

By this time the inspector had paced out the route to school with a measuring wheel. The local authority decided, after all, that a school taxi service would be provided. Mr Light, a kind, elderly man of few words, was employed to do the run for the five children in Bromley. My reprieve was at an end.

I was one of the first children to be collected. After that, Mr Light went to pick up children from the outlying farms, returning via Bromley to the main village. This route caused me much distress. From the moment I got in the car, I politely asked the thickset back of Mr Light's neck if he would please take me home, as I would much rather spend the day there. When, after some minutes, I saw us approaching Bromley Stores, I'd begin thanking him for his kindness, only to be thrown into despair as we sailed past the shop door. I remember trying to make the car stop by pushing my feet hard against the back of the seat in front of me. When this failed, I started sobbing and my tears carried on into the school day.

My first teacher was an uncompromising lady. Such grief as mine met with no sympathy and I was promptly dumped on a chair behind the clothes airer to be as much out of sight and mind as possible. This time-out area was used extensively. One girl was left there all afternoon as she would persist in crying. It was only on reaching home that it was realised that she had broken her finger.

I chiefly remember this teacher by her string of pearls and the silky sheen of her hand-knitted pale green or beige cardigans. Her classroom was an orderly, pleasant place to be. The sandpit was a real joy, as was the Wendy house full of dressing up clothes. Most children also loved the large slide arching over the other toys. I found the height of it very frightening, though, and my only pleasure was that of relief at having landed safely at the bottom.

Learning to mix with other children was a hard lesson for me. Getting a tiny, pocket-size doll to take to school, like the other girls, helped a lot. There were so few children that quite often we all played together in large games of stick-in-the-mud or football, which I enjoyed.

Soon after starting school we had a medical, during which the kindly district nurse discovered that I was extremely short-sighted. She was so concerned that she drove me straight home to discuss the problem with my parents. No one had guessed my handicap. My delight in reading and looking at books had been seen as a sign of intelligence, rather than as an escape valve for someone who could focus on very little else.

I was soon fitted with little, round, wire National Health Service glasses with pink bits of plastic stuck on here and there. I didn't care what they looked like. I was overwhelmed, especially by trees, as I had no idea how

Starting school

beautiful they were. I was also quite frightened when I first wore them at home, as perspectives ganged up on me, making floors appear to rise up and slant at extraordinary angles. This effect soon faded and I was left with the joy of seeing the loveliness of the countryside into which we had moved. My favourite spot was perching on the sill of my parents' bedroom window. Looking out over the lichened tiles of the shop roof, cushioned with moss, there was a breathtaking quilt of fields and hedgerows, of magpies strutting about, of swallows dipping and soaring, of lanes that twisted on forever. Best of all was the hill topped with a copse of trees, which could be spotted for miles around and which always meant home to me when I was travelling back from a distance.

I remember the first day of going to school in glasses. I felt a little shy, a little proud and I longed to see every last detail sharply and clearly. A kind girl in my class called Nancy took one look at me and led me off to a quiet bit of the playground. 'I don't want to worry you, Christine. I think you look very nice in your glasses. Pink suits you. Still, I really think you need to talk to my cousin Helen. She wears glasses too and, well, maybe there are some things you need to know.' Saying no more, she led me off to her big cousin for advice. Helen was very kind too and gently warned me that some children might enjoy bullying me more now but that glasses were important and I was to try not to mind too much.

Along Featherbed Lane

I thought they were exaggerating but, sure enough, that poor little pair of glasses brought down the bullies like crows to a carcass. I was very large for my age but the bullies seemed like giantesses. Having noticed me, they must have found me good prey. Every morning, in the teacher-less time between the taxi dropping us off and school beginning, I was their entertainment. My maths homework, my bag and my name were hurled around the empty classroom and twisted with hatred. Early on, I decided I would not give them the satisfaction of seeing how much they upset me, so I sat tight-lipped and prim, waiting out the time of torment.

Home was a different matter. After a day at school, I had in Mum and Dad an audience waiting to praise my achievements to the skies and to commiserate with my disappointments. I relived the joy or pain of each moment so vividly that my tale was accompanied by a rapid alternation of tears and beaming smiles.

Much more important than the bullying my glasses brought, however, was the gaining of my first best friend, for that was what Nancy became and stayed throughout our time at Stanton Drew School. She was and still is as good, kind and true a friend as I could ever wish to have. She overlooked the fact that I 'talked like a dictionary'. She didn't mind that I was absolutely hopeless at handstands, cartwheels and turning somersaults over high metal bars, things that all the other girls did with grace and ease. She encouraged my feeble attempts on the apparatus and we played hopscotch and skipping but

Starting school

mostly just chatted. Nancy had three brothers, a sister and quite a few cousins at the school, so from now on the playground became a friendlier place, in which I was no longer alone.

Chapter 4: Neighbours

Soon after we arrived, one of the locals pointed out that it would be a good seven years before anyone would begin to think of us as villagers. We found out that this was no exaggeration. Fortunately, though, running the shop provided a good way of making the acquaintance of many of the residents.

In the adjoining house was dear Mrs Ashley, a kind, gentle old lady, after whom I named my favourite teddy bear. She was cared for by her daughter, Mrs Tovey, a very friendly and chatty person. Fortunately, all the people who lived in the row of Bromley Villas were pleasant. The open-plan gardens could have made life difficult otherwise.

Mr and Mrs Tovey and their son Geoff kept pigs in the corrugated and stone-built sties in the garden of the house at the opposite end of our row. The older pigs grazed contentedly in the field behind the far end of our garden, snuffling up fallen apples as a treat. One evening, Mr Tovey rushed into our shop, red-faced and panting a little.

'Not long now until you close for the evening is it, Mr Longhurst? Just as soon as you do, I'd like you all to come along to our back gate. We've got something special to show you.' Without any further explanation, he opened the shop door again and was gone.

'I don't think we've got any choice but to do as Mr Tovey asks,' Mum reflected. 'They're very good

Neighbours

neighbours and it must be a matter of importance for him to suddenly come around like that. He seemed quite out of breath. I hope everything is all right.'

Just after eight o'clock, we presented ourselves at the gate as requested. Mrs Tovey was looking out for us from her kitchen window. 'Come on, my dears, come on in. I expect Mr Tovey told you all about them already. Such a beautiful litter as we haven't had for many a long year.' Mr and Mrs Tovey proudly took us on a tour of the sties to see the new mum and her row of tiny, pink, noisy babies. Even the larger, muddier teenage pigs seemed good-humoured and loveable.

'Oh, Mrs Tovey,' Mum would exclaim at each sty we passed, 'these pigs of yours are absolutely gorgeous and as for those piglets, I don't know when I've seen anything so sweet.' Dad asked Mr Tovey sensible questions about foodstuff and bedding and listened intently to the answers. However, he shuffled a little on legs that were becoming painfully tired with all the standing. I said very little but my eyes were shining with excitement. One feature of these pigs' diet was novel. Since Mr Tovey worked during the day for a local crisp firm, they gave him all the out of date packets. So alongside the squeals and snufflings was the sound of crisp packets being trampled to bursting by greedy little pigs. On our way back home, Mrs Tovey also showed us the hood of her well in which, year after year, a family of blue tits nested.

Along Featherbed Lane

These pigs, almost more than anything else, made us feel that we were experiencing country life. Their squeals and grunts formed a constant background noise in our garden, along with the velvet cooing of wood pigeons and the clear, sweet songs of blackbird and thrush. There was even a cheeky starling, who sat on our roof and mimicked everything in earshot, including a cat mewing and Mum's rather loud and refined laugh.

In practical ways also we shared in the joys of having nearby pigs. All leftover food was dumped into the pigswill canister left outside our back door and collected each day by Geoff. In return, we received every now and then a heap of manure to enrich still further the good, black soil of Bromley.

Conversations with Mrs Tovey were often worth repeating. If any complaint was to be made, they always began 'Mother said...'. In this very gentle and roundabout way, 'Mother' would point out the thinness of the walls with a 'Surely that can't be Mrs Longhurst practising her piano so late at night?' She also highlighted the racket I made when I was in a temper with the comment 'Mother said, "I wonder if that Christine has gone and got herself locked in somewhere to be making all that banging and shouting."'

Thankfully such complaints were rare. Mrs Tovey was a kind-hearted neighbour with a good sense of humour. When, in later years, Dad's sight became badly obscured by cataracts, even trips to the outside toilet became quite hazardous. He was surprised by how often

Neighbours

Mrs Tovey, wearing her characteristic royal blue overall, was standing near her back door. He was even more surprised and rather hurt that she no longer bothered to reply to his cheery 'Good morning!' This puzzled us all until one day when he amazed Mum, who was with him, by greeting Mrs Tovey's blue bucket. This story was too good to keep to ourselves. When Mrs Tovey heard it, she laughed until she cried. 'Oh Mr Longhurst,' she eventually choked out, 'I know I've always been short but I've never been mistaken for a bucket before!'

Soon after we moved to Bromley, Mrs Tovey kindly offered to keep me company on the walk down the hill for the fortnightly visits of the mobile library. I fetched as many books as I could stagger home with. First I picked big print westerns, thrillers or war books for Dad. Then I looked for memoirs, historical novels or classics for Mum. This was trickier, however, as there were so many possible books to choose from. Perfecting my choices took a while. One visit I got very excited at the look of a Stanley Gibbons catalogue. I'm not sure why I thought this would please Mum so much, since she wasn't really interested in stamps, but I was convinced that this was a great choice. So much so that, due to its immense weight, this was the only book I managed to fetch her. Poor Mum was duly delighted all fortnight long. However, when the library day came round eventually, she did mention that maybe I shouldn't strain myself by trying to bring volume two home and that a few Miss Read or Paul Gallico books would make a nice

Along Featherbed Lane

change. Once I had a good armful for Mum and Dad, I piled up my choices. My best ever choice was *Huckleberry Finn,* which coincided with me having a very bad attack of the measles. I giggled my way through the high fevers and discomfort with Mum and Dad taking it in turns to perch on the edge of my bed and read chapters to me.

Another villager whose friendship and kindness enriched our lives was our cleaner Mrs Kingston. She came several times a week to help Mum with the heavier cleaning and the washing. Mum harked back to a time when her family had housemaids so, whatever our finances, a domestic help was a necessity. Mrs Kingston trudged up the hill to our shop pushing her bike, all neatly bundled up in her buttoned-up mac tied at the waist and a headscarf which framed a face creased and twinkling with smiles. It always tickled her how very far down the hill she could begin to hear Mum's voice and laugh.

To us, newcomers to the village, her presence was as welcome as that of the robin coaxed by crumbs to include our garden in his territory. Eager, bright-eyed, head tilted in watchfulness, he followed our attempts at gardening with gently patronising encouragement. Mrs Kingston accepted small gifts of food naturally and without thanks, as part of the order of things. 'I'll take it off your hands if you want,' she would murmur in response. However, she cherished us, lending me her precious bicycle to practise my wobbling on, praising my singing as being just like the singer on the record

Neighbours

and bringing scraps of village gossip to our windswept hamlet.

Life among such neighbours was comfortable and easy-going. In this part of Somerset, men were often referred to as 'her' and 'she' and so farmers' wives spoke indulgently of their stay-on-the-farm husbands as if they were naughty little girls. 'Her do be doing this!' or 'What! Bain't she done that yet vor ye?' would ring out from the back seats of the bus amid gales of laughter.

Not all contact with neighbours was this kindly though. In the detached house next to us lived a boy of my age who saw the Longhursts as suitable prey. Our Cox's Orange Pippin apples were peppered with airgun pellets. Our broad beans were used as rifle range practice, until all the slender stems had been felled. With a final flourish, he punched a pellet into the lower part of our huge water butt, wasting the precious water in a fine spurt. I'd had enough. I stamped through the house and burst into the shop, demanding a packet of chewing gum. Filling my mouth with sugar-coated pellets, I chewed my way savagely back through the house into the backyard. I covered the leak with the large blob of gum, smearing down the edges to form a seal. Mercifully it worked and the gum slowly hardened and weathered into one with the dull grey metal of the water butt. His reign of mischief against us had lost some of its power.

Mostly though, life was slow-paced and content with its lot. Days passed sleepily and seasons gently nudged each other when it was their turn and no one

Along Featherbed Lane

seemed to mind how long things took. Cars waited patiently in the midst of a herd of cows being moved along the road from one field to another. I even remember three of our cats, who had followed Jonathan, Patrick and me the 100 yards up the road to the bus stop, spreading themselves out and trotting back down the road ahead of the weekly bus to Bristol. No horn was sounded, no one shouted or swore, we just drove slowly. Jonathan, Patrick and I shrank down in our seats as, one by one, the cats all trooped into our shop, finally allowing the bus and us with it on our way.

Chapter 5: Cats and kittens

One evening, just as we were sitting down to tea, the bell rang and, as usual, Dad headed for the shop. I was amazed when, a few moments later, he reappeared along with Mr Stevens, a local farmer, who had a little bundle wrapped up in his arms. He gently placed it down on the rug near the open fire and out tottered a grey and white kitten. Whilst I nestled the kitten in the corner of my arm and named him Timothy, Mum fretted after the departing form of Mr Stevens. 'Why tonight of all nights? Why did I have to buy that repulsive-looking smoked cod? We never have visitors and then tonight one pops in when I've just dished up the most hideous meal I've ever cooked!' Plates of vibrant yellow cod, boiled potatoes and tinned tomatoes certainly did no justice to Mum's lovely cooking. However, for me, nothing could take away the joy of having my first kitten.

Timothy grew into a beautiful cat but, as he did so, it became apparent that we had been mistaken. 'He' was definitely expecting a litter of kittens and was hastily renamed Timoshe. Her kittens arrived late one evening during a blizzard. Timoshe was petrified by the whole experience and, without stopping to feed or care for her new family, she dodged between Dad's feet as he returned from the outside toilet and made her escape into the storm. As soon as it became obvious that she was not about to rush back to her babies, Mum took charge. The cardboard box full of kittens was brought from the cold

Along Featherbed Lane

kitchen to in front of the living-room fire. Even so, the tiny creatures were shivering and fumbling blindly around the box, mewing for a mother's care. We fed them on milk diluted with warm water from the tips of our little fingers until they were snoozy and satisfied. Then, to comfort them to sleep, Mum wrapped a warm hot water bottle in an old fleecy cardigan of mine. Cuddled down on this, one by one the kittens soon fell asleep.

Timoshe came back the next morning and grudgingly took on the role of motherhood. However, she was restless and uneasy and, once these kittens had been given away, she left herself. I called her for breakfast and supper day after day for months, until I was worn down with sadness. A new kitten was bought and Thomas, a four-square and determined tabby, soon became lord and master of the local cats. As a kitten he was jealous of the amount of time I spent cuddling my teddy bears and we came in from the garden one day to find him fast asleep on the chest of my enormous 'Big Ted', his forepaws weary from scratching his rival.

Thomas loved standing under the cheeseboard in the shop waiting for snippets of cheese or circling in a strong current around our legs until we shared our crisps with him. A little after Thomas arrived we were given a tiny, greyish tabby kitten with dainty white bib, paws and nose, who I named Tiggy. 'Poor little mite!' Mum would say, 'She's much too young to have been taken away from her mother. Still, Chrissie, she seems to have picked on you to take her place, so you must give her all the love

Cats and kittens

and time she needs.' Sure enough, Tiggy spent hours on my lap, snuggling purrily into the comforting warmth of my cardigan sleeves. These soon became shredded, as she was constantly kneading the inside of my elbow with her minute paws.

Tiggy and Thomas became firm friends in love and mischief. We became puzzled about how often one of us would seem to carelessly leave the back door ajar, allowing the cats access. It remained a mystery until one day when Mum came up the garden quietly and saw the cats in action. Whilst Tiggy jumped onto the back-room windowsill and reached over to press down the latch on the outside of the back door, Thomas put his head down and pushed hard against the door, edging it open enough for them to slip in. Thomas's love of food was always a powerful temptation for him. One day our fishmonger, having paid his weekly visit, surprised us by returning soon after. This delivery was even more of a surprise, as instead of a basket of wet fish, he appeared with a ruffled tomcat under his arm. Thomas had managed to stow away for a heavenly ride down to the village.

As she grew up, Tiggy changed from treating me as her mother to thinking of me as her kitten. Every morning, I'd awake to the gentle rasping of her tongue over my face. If this didn't make me open my eyes, she would pat me on the nose with her paw until I sat up and tickled her behind the ears.

Tiggy proved to be a good mother. She liked to have Mum on hand as honorary midwife when the kittens

Along Featherbed Lane

were born. For a few days' before, you'd find Tiggy squeezing herself into any box she could find, no matter how small, just to see if it would prove to be a suitable nest for her kittens. We would get a nice clean box ready, lined with newspaper and an old cardigan, and Tiggy would try it out, turning herself around for comfort and sniffing into the corners. When all was ready for the birth, Tiggy liked to have the box lid folded shut. After each kitten was born, her head popped up briefly so that Mum could stroke her and tell her what a wonderful cat she was, before she disappeared again for the next push. Mum chattered away soothingly throughout, lavishing praise on Tiggy's head each time it appeared in tired triumph.

Tiggy trusted us with her kittens, so we had the joy of watching them from their first blind days until their eyelids gradually peeled open to show their deep blue eyes. As their legs grew stronger and they wanted more than milk and sleep, they grew adventurous and managed to kick and scrabble their way out of their box to explore the kitchen with its old raffia rug and earth box. We never gave our kittens away until they were old enough to eat and drink from saucers. Under our watchful eyes, they were also allowed into the garden. They loved playing there, jumping out at one another with stiff legs from behind clumps of weeds, but inevitably they all made a rush for the earth box as soon as they came back in. Very gently we helped them to dig holes in the soft soil in the garden until they understood.

Cats and kittens

Tiggy also liked to coach them in hunting and would smuggle a bird into the house, deftly catching it in front of her eager-eyed pupils. Both adult cats were excellent hunters but only when they wanted to be. For some reason, a field mouse that strayed into our shop was of no interest to them. Dad eventually caught it himself and showed it to Tiggy and Thomas before throwing them out with mutterings of 'lazy, incompetent, good-for-nothing cats' ringing in their ears. By the following morning, our back step was covered with an enormous dead rat, which they must have caught in the pigsties. After that, every now and again, long, hideously bald rats' tails would be left on our back step as trophies, just in case we should ever again dare to doubt their prowess as hunters.

By the time that Tiggy's kittens were a few weeks old, they were utterly adorable and full of mischief. They swung on the curtains, they ran up and down the piano keys and, on cold evenings, they climbed up the outside of the wire fireguard to toast their tummies. Tiggy was loving and tolerant of their pranks. Usually, any kitten who went too far was cuffed and pinned down for a long wash.

Only one proved too much for this good mother. Jeremy was naughty and disobedient to Tiggy, scratching and squirming away from any attempt of hers to keep him in check. To us spectators, he was just a delightful little show-off. One afternoon Tiggy had had enough. Getting him by the scruff of the neck, she carried him up the steps

Along Featherbed Lane

out of the kitchen, through the dining room, along the hall and down into the living room, where she dropped him huffily at Mum's feet. Stretching herself, she then returned with dignity to look after her good kittens. Mum and I had a wonderful time looking after this little mischief. Finally, before his bedtime feed, Tiggy returned for him. Whether this punishment improved Jeremy's behaviour or whether Tiggy just missed him too much, I don't know, but we were never asked to 'babysit' again.

Chapter 6: Ill health

During our first year at Bromley came a day that changed my parents' lives forever. I arrived home from school to find Mum and Patrick waiting for me in the shop. Dad was nowhere to be seen. Gently, they explained that he had gone to hospital in an ambulance. He had been in a lot of pain because there was a clot of blood in his leg. The clot was so bad that, if they couldn't shift it, he would have to lose his leg. Mum told me how Patrick had stayed brave and strong and even managed to cheer them up with a joke about Dad being like Long John Silver. She was upset that the doctor had been quite sharp with him over this and couldn't believe that he hadn't seen the love, care and pain behind the teasing.

Still, Dad came home quite quickly and life should have gone back to normal but it didn't. Something was wrong but it was hard to say what. Thankfully, Mum shared her worries with an elderly neighbour, Mrs Bourne, who had been a nurse. She offered to come and take a look at Dad and Mum gratefully accepted. This kind offer, on an evening shortly before Christmas, saved his life. Mrs Bourne realised how desperately ill he was and borrowed our telephone to call for an ambulance. Whilst all this was happening, the family had been gathered around the television watching The Lost World. Patrick had been particularly excited about seeing this, as it was one of his favourite books. Full of elated terror, I didn't understand the real-life drama that was unfolding

Along Featherbed Lane

around me and did not want to be interrupted. 'You must come and wave Daddy goodbye!' Mum said for the second time, taking me firmly by the hand and leading me out to where the ambulance doors were swallowing him up, out of my sight. I wept angry, frustrated tears. I had no idea that the clot from his leg had moved into his lungs and was edging its way towards his heart. Dad's life hung on by the thinnest of threads.

Since it seemed likely that I might never see Dad again, Mum got special permission for me to visit him at Southmead Hospital. It was terrifying to see Dad so gaunt and threaded through with tubes. These images haunted me in nightmares for weeks and the fear of Dad dying was a black cloud in the sunshine of my childhood. Sometimes it drew near enough to cast shadows. Sometimes it moved away but it would never go completely.

It now became obvious that Dad, even if he recovered, would be an invalid. This was some challenge to a self-employed workaholic. Mum worked hard to stay brave. One conversation with Dad, however, moved her very much. As the bell rang for the end of visiting hours, he said as a closing thought to her, 'You know, Joan, money isn't everything.' This, from the man who had worked all day and half the night for years to build up his precious toyshop, was too much for Mum. As soon as she and Jonathan got outside the hospital ward, she broke down and shed the torrent of tears that had been building

Ill health

up behind the floodgates. Soon afterwards, though, she was able to laugh about this, even with Dad.

Being constantly together was no problem for Mum and Dad. Mum hated being alone. The aspect of Dad's new status as an invalid that did cause great concern, though, was who would run the shop. Dad was certainly not able to, especially in the early years of his illness. In later times, he used to sit for long hours there, making rugs or doing crosswords and serving the odd customer. Mum hated the thought of facing the world over the counter but Patrick boosted her confidence with endless encouragement and eventually won her round to helping there. Since September Patrick had been studying Maths at St John's College, Oxford, following in Jonathan's footsteps. Although his Open Scholarship had been so hard-won, he showed amazing generosity by considering giving up his place to stay at home and look after us. Thankfully Dr Jones, the wonderfully supportive and kind senior doctor from the surgery at Chew Magna, strongly advised against this.

Mum was never wholly at ease in the shop but she managed well. Always a mine of information on medical matters and genuinely interested in people and their problems, she had her own gifts to bring to the role of shopkeeper.

It seemed a great blessing that the manager of our toyshop in Bristol was so willing to cope on his own during our family crisis. We were assured, 'Leave me to manage here, Mrs Longhurst. Don't worry about a thing. I'll take care of it for you and poor Mr Longhurst.'

Sadly the manager, left to his own devices without guidance from Mum, failed to manage the business well for us. Unsupervised, the profits from the shop dwindled away, along with the customers and the goodwill built up lovingly and carefully over the years by Dad. The shop itself needed to be sold to pay off debts to our suppliers. However, although the manager was fired from his post, he and his family refused to move out of the house of which the shop was simply the converted front room. With these hostile sitting tenants, we had no chance of selling the property and business, so our crippled finances collapsed still further. Patrick spent the summer holiday running the shop, working hard to redeem the hopeless mess. When he needed to return to St John's College for the new term, he got a friend of his first girlfriend Carol to take over the job for him. Patrick had chosen well. Nick Hillier, who played saxophone for the jazz band Henry's Bootblacks, turned out to be a good friend to our family. He recognised the need for us to sell and set out to make this possible, even though by so doing he would be depriving himself of a job. The only access that Nick and his Saturday assistant had to the house was for using the bathroom. Nick had noticed how much annoyance these toilet trips caused if they coincided with a mealtime. Needless to say, this spurred a great many 'ill-timed' visits until our tenants finally decided to move.

Ill health

We now had virtually no money apart from £70 in Mum's Post Office account. Dad was an invalid, unable to work, and Bromley Stores would never provide us with much more than pocket money and food for ourselves at wholesale prices.

Such a turn of events could have left my parents twisted with bitterness. It did not. As I remember it, our chief feelings were of enormous relief that Dad had survived and the security of being together. Dad was an optimist and a staunch believer that things turned out the way they were meant to. Nightly, Dad and Mum knelt on either side of their bed in silent prayer. Dad's faith in God's providential care sustained him then and throughout the rest of his life.

Integrity was a key quality of my parents' character and one which poverty did not steal from them. One incident illustrated this characteristic particularly well. Buying self-employment stamps had become a hardship and Mum and Dad had to save very hard to have enough money to send Jonathan off to Bristol to buy a few months' worth of them. This meant a long day in Bristol for Jonathan, as buses were few and far between. When he finally arrived home, weary from waiting in the bus depot with children grizzling with tiredness and drunks slumped over the railings, he would hand over the precious stamps and carefully saved change. However, on this occasion, instead of receiving thanks, Jonathan was stunned by Dad's reaction. 'What on earth...?' he began. 'There's something mighty strange here, Joan. There must be several years of stamps here, worth a small fortune. How on earth did you come back with this lot, Jonathan?'

Jonathan relived the scene in the Post Office for us. The young girl assistant had carefully divided the sheet of stamps into two unequal parts and handed one portion to him, along with the two shillings and sixpence of change. 'You know what must have happened, don't you?' Mum chipped in. 'Poor little thing must have got the two sheets muddled and given you the remainder. I'm so sorry, Jon, but you're going to have to take these back and sort it out with that assistant.'

Whatever Jonathan may have thought about the wisdom of handing back this apparent godsend, when Mum and Dad were so desperately short of money, he knew that they were adamant and so he went. What he had not reckoned upon was the reaction of the young assistant when she recognised him and realised that he was bringing back the stamps. Tears started pouring down her face as she explained how angry the manager had been with her for having her till down so badly at the end of the day and how she had been told that she must make up the loss from her wages. Jonathan mentioned that she had insisted on jotting down his name and address but this detail got lost in the sense of joy and relief that my parents were feeling on knowing that their insistence on returning the stamps had made such a difference.

Ill health

A few days later a parcel arrived at the shop. 'That's funny,' Mum commented as she tore off the brown wrapping paper, 'I don't recognise the handwriting at all but it's got a Bristol postmark.' Inside she found a thank you note from the assistant and underneath this a large, square, golden box of chocolates. 'Terry's All Gold,' Mum exclaimed with a little gasp. 'I haven't had these in years. What a lovely treat and how very kind of her. I must say I don't remember the time I saw such a beautiful box of chocolates.' Never have chocolates tasted so rich and wonderful. To my surprise and delight, when we had eaten the top layer, Dad pulled out a golden drawer from the bottom of the box to reveal another whole harvest of chocolates.

I only have a few memories of Dad before his illness. The best is of him carrying me around our toyshop at night to say goodnight to all my favourite toys. We always ended up with a plastic corgi raised on his haunches to beg. Such days were gone for good. Dad was nearly always Dad in an armchair, with his feet raised on a pouffe and his legs uncrossed, whenever we reminded him. From there, he did everything he could to keep his mind active: crosswords, puzzles, reading war stories and making rugs. These rugs were wonderful expressions of Dad's artistry and his love for us. Each was made specially with a room or person in mind. Once Dad got into the swing of making them, he took great pleasure in using his own designs, meticulously calculating the number of available stitches in any colour from his bundle of offcuts.

Dad took a particular interest in current affairs, reading his Daily Telegraph avidly and watching or listening every day to news bulletins at 8 am, 1 pm, 6 pm, 9 pm and, if possible, 10 pm as well. The Budget was also listened to in rapt attention as long as broadcasts lasted, much to my dismay.

Although Dad's body let him down so early, his mind remained alert for the rest of his life, full of wit, wisdom and intellectual curiosity. Never moaning about the limitations imposed on him by his illness, Dad was grateful for any small improvement or degree of strength. As the years went by and he spent less time sleeping away the day, he took great pride in doing household jobs like ironing, carpet sweeping and preparing salad vegetables to perfection. Old cotton sheets were ironed and folded with precision, the carpet sweeper was emptied and dusted out daily and our lettuce and raw cabbage were always finely and evenly shredded. No job was ever rushed or done in a slipshod way by Dad.

Time spent with Dad was always interesting. His views were informed and intelligent and he was also a great listener and good at giving encouragement and praise. He was a wonderful teacher for those subjects I found most difficult. It was Dad who coached me on my times tables whilst I sat on the shop counter, dangling my legs and looking out of the tiny side window for inspiration. My lack of knowledge of the times tables

Ill health

was a strange consequence of my good behaviour in Mrs Long's class, since learning them was reserved as a punishment. With knitting I had a complete blind spot, no matter how much Mum tried to teach me. Dad got me started by pretending to show me how to do it but deliberately getting everything so hopelessly wrong that I was compelled to remember what Mum had been painstakingly showing me, in order to put him right.

As a doting husband and father, Dad was also a great tease. Standard jokes and ditties were repeated at entirely predictable moments. If Mum ever said 'I'm only joking,' the response 'Really? I thought you were Joanie Longhurst!' was inevitable. If a hot, milky drink was offered, the comment was always 'Hor-likes it very much!' And so on and on, amid the family's groans. Way back, behind those pebble glasses, Dad's bright blue eyes were twinkling at us.

Chapter 7: Managing

Mum was a highly intelligent, resourceful and courageous woman. She took sudden poverty on board as a creative challenge. As a young woman in the Second World War, she had learnt the ability to 'make do and mend' and this stood her in good stead. Nothing was wasted or thrown away.

Generosity also played a big part in keeping us afloat. My brothers stretched their university grants in order to pay the rental on a television for us. My sisters-in-law to be, Judith and Laura, were also very kind in making much-needed summer dresses for me and Laura also passed down a beautifully warm green winter coat to me. My great-aunts Nem and Dolly sent a parcel of lace petticoats. My Mum handled each one with respect, carefully unfolding and wondering over the prettiness of the deep borders of white or cream lace. Ignoring the shop labels, she treated them with delight, as family heirlooms.

Not having enough money to buy clothes inspired Mum to develop her knitting and sewing skills. Parcels of remnants and scraps were sent for. Very inexpensive, the former 'lucky dip' collection of lengths of material made up into some pretty dresses. The scraps were used to make frocks for my favourite dolls. This must have been very fiddly and time-consuming work for Mum, but it certainly provided me with many hours of entertainment and pleasure. I was extremely fortunate to

Managing

have seemingly endless time and love available from both Mum and Dad, gifts more precious than anything. Praise and encouragement to do well were always overflowing. As far as Mum and Dad were concerned, Jonathan, Patrick and I were capable of doing anything we wanted to do and we all did our best to live up to their partiality and pride.

Our home at Bromley had a 100 foot long strip of garden and this was put to good use. It was Mum's proud boast that, apart from potatoes and, of course, the more exotic fruits like oranges and bananas, we grew all our own fruit and vegetables.

There were already two large apple trees, a tree of miniature apples, a cantankerous plum tree, a patch of raspberry canes, a bed of strawberry plants and some blackcurrant and gooseberry bushes. Mum added redcurrant bushes and a dear little Cox's Orange Pippin tree.

In the summer we ate like kings, with large bowls of either strawberries or raspberries each day. The surplus was frozen down or turned into jams, jellies or wine. The kitchen stool was turned upside down and the four corners of a muslin square tied one to each leg. Then, very carefully, the stewed fruit was poured into the centre of the cloth and allowed to drip slowly through into a large china mixing bowl below.

Home-brewed wines fermented well in the cupboard under the stairs, which backed onto Mrs Ashley's living-room fireplace. We also grew a large box of mushrooms in there and these flourished with daily pickings until Mrs Ashley and Mrs Tovey had a little holiday and the sudden cold finished them off.

In our sitting room was a large oak sideboard. This was stacked to brimming with jars of home-made jams and pickles. My favourite meals were always the cold ones, where a few plump slices of ham or a generous chunk of tasty Cheddar and some bread and butter served as the excuse for a feast of pickled delights. Shallots, red cabbage, sliced beetroot, piccalilli and apple, gooseberry, green tomato, runner bean and autumn chutney were ranked on the table, ready to be enjoyed.

As well as the traditional vegetables—lettuces, tomatoes, broad beans, runner and dwarf beans, cauliflowers, spring greens, Brussels sprouts, leeks, carrots and onions—Mum tried her hand at some more unusual ones. For many years we grew marrows and pumpkins. One hot summer, we even had a large square bed of sweetcorn. Chives, mint and parsley flavoured our food and there was still some room left for primulas, tulips, nasturtiums, roses and the odd patch of lawn.

Mum had little strength for heavy gardening. Five or so years after we moved in, our doctor realised that Mum's heart had a faulty valve that caused it to beat irregularly, especially if she exerted herself or became too stressed. It seemed that this problem dated back to an attack of rheumatic fever when she was at boarding school as a little girl. Until our doctor's discovery, her difficulty in dealing with some situations had been

Managing

dismissed as 'nerves'. Dad had always tried to fortify her by opposing this view with the assertion that she hadn't got a nerve in her body. Discovering a good, solid, physical reason for some of her problems was a great source of relief to them both.

What Mum lacked in stamina, she made up for in determination. Every day we had a late lunch hour when the shop was closed. We actually ate at an earlier time, fitting in the food between the random customers. Lunchtime was gardening hour, later extended to an hour and a half. With her trowel, Mum dug up her daily two bucketfuls of weeds and masterminded the care of her plants. One day, after gardening, Mum gave a little scream as she washed her hands. The diamond had fallen out of her engagement ring. After a few minutes of despair, she tied on her headscarf and folded her arms stubbornly. 'I'll be back when I've found it,' she said firmly. Eventually she returned triumphant. Miraculously, she had spotted the tiny stone on the path below the Peace rose, even though it was hiding with its sparkling side to the earth.

Jonathan and Patrick provided energetic help in the garden on their visits home. They attacked the big jobs, like cutting the hedges and trying to win back the far end of the garden from an ever-flowing sea of nettles and ground elder. Meanwhile, I learnt how to use a spade, fork, rake and hoe and prepared the ground between the old trees for Mum to plant out her next season of vegetables. I also loved harvesting the soft fruits, a job

Along Featherbed Lane

that I shared with Dad as he grew strong enough to join in. It was easy to fill the old metal colander to the brim with raspberries, wending your way through the paths that threaded through the large patch of canes.

Once the luscious summer fruits had passed, there was autumn to look forward to. Apples rarely had to be harvested from the trees. Sharp winds at night brought them down sooner than we would have picked them. The ground beneath was usually soft, though, so relatively little damage was done. Armed with Mum's wicker basket, I gathered up every windfall, piling them up on the kitchen floor for Mum's inspection. The very best were wrapped in newspaper and stored in cardboard boxes in the bedrooms. The bruised were kept in the kitchen for stewing or eating raw. The really battered ones were quickly turned into chutney or jam.

One year a particularly vicious wind brought down nearly the whole crop in a night. The kitchen was knee-deep in apples and even Mum ran out of ideas for using them up. Giving them away to neighbours was hopeless, as the whole village was awash in windfall fruit. Mum wanted to give them to the poor but, on making enquiries, was told that no one in the Chew Valley went hungry: there was always plenty of food to go around. Despite a great shortage of money, that was certainly true for us too. Mum finally rang up a Bristol branch of the Salvation Army. They were laying on a harvest supper for a hall full of destitute people and were very pleased to collect a van's worth of apples to make pies for dessert.

Managing

The bounty of our garden provided more than enough for us. It also gave enough for invaluable swaps of produce. Despite Thomas's misbehaviour, our very kind-hearted fishmonger traded us fresh fish for ice-cream tubs of gooseberries. It also made entertaining possible. One day Jonathan unexpectedly brought home a handful of friends from university. Mum was very chuffed to be able to provide a luxurious afternoon tea of large bowls of strawberries and raspberries, generously laced with castor sugar and cream, along with slices of shortbread and glasses of lemonade.

Although the vast majority of the garden was used for growing fruit and vegetables, it was far more than an allotment. For me, it was a place of enchantment and delight, a shady maze of raspberry canes and bushes, where imagination made anything possible. Best of all was my swing. It was sawn from a plank of wood and fixed by sturdy, waxed ropes to one of our apple trees. I cannot begin to reckon up the number of hours I spent playing on that swing, soaring far into the deep blue sky, or sitting astride it as Maid Marian riding through Sherwood Forest.

Screened from our neighbours' gaze by a thicket of blackcurrant bushes, the grassy patch of ground near my swing was my favourite part of the garden. It was also the scene of our Sunday afternoon family picnics. Mum adored picnics. When a picnic had had to be abandoned because of the rain when she was a girl, my Grandma had

Along Featherbed Lane

taken Mum and her little brother and sister for a picnic in her bedroom. My Mum was equally determined.

Old folding garden chairs were carried down the garden for Mum and Dad and I perched on my swing. Marmite sandwiches first, then crisps, cans of fizzy drink and our favourite chocolate bars. Such teas were an enormous treat, apart from the Marmite sandwiches, which never tasted quite as good as they did indoors.

Unfortunately, Dad was on a strict 1000 calories a day diet following his illness. Mum took this very seriously, counting calories precisely. The calorific content of such a picnic tea proved quite a shock to her when she tallied up afterwards. 'Oh, Chrissie, what I am going to do? That poor man has only got five calories left for the rest of the day!' When it was time for supper, Dad was horrified to find nothing but a single lettuce leaf on his plate. Thankfully, Mum relented and allowed Dad a slice of bread and butter and a sliver of ham, on condition that he kept to his daily helping of calories from then on.

Dad did lose some weight but he took little pleasure in this. For him, food was a wonderful ritual and the dietician a monster to be avoided at all costs. He relished every meal, no matter how simple or repetitive. Mum used to laugh about the fact that, when they first got married, Dad had said that she could cook him stew followed by stewed apples and custard every day if she liked and he'd be quite happy. Certainly, at the end of every meal, Dad would neatly lay down his knife and fork side by side, wipe the corner of his mouth with his

Managing

napkin and turn to Mum with shining eyes and an apt compliment. 'Well, Joan, you've excelled yourself again. That was the tastiest ham I've ever had.'

Mum enjoyed dieting far more than Dad and was very competitive about the results of their weekly weigh-in. During her second pregnancy, Mum had suffered from toxaemia. In those days, the treatment was to cut out all protein from the mother's diet, even the small amount found in peas and beans. After weeks of cabbage soup, her doctor finally relented over Christmas dinner and said that she could have a tiny square of turkey breast as a treat. The memory of such hardship brought tears to Mum's eyes, though these were soon chased away by the thought that her strange diet might have given baby Patrick his beautiful complexion and golden curls. However, once he was born, Mum was left gaunt and suffering from post-natal depression. Her beloved elderly doctor gave instructions that she was never to go on a diet again.

Mum was always very obedient to the decrees of a doctor, even when common sense might have told her that enough was enough. Her weight soared up to over sixteen stone by the time I was born thirteen years later and stayed there throughout the early years of my life. Mercifully, Mum's doctor at Bromley managed to assure her that losing weight would be a wise move. Mum had a very sweet tooth and could not bear the thought of giving up her hot milky drinks spiked with spoonfuls of both sugar and glucose or her reviving chunks of Turkish

Along Featherbed Lane

Delight. However, she decided to cut down on fat and carbohydrates and did so with strict self-discipline. Crispbreads and cottage cheese with a sliver of Edam became Mum's staple lunch, followed by half a grapefruit crusty with white sugar. She ate lean meat and small helpings of potato. Steadily the pounds came off until she finally lost over four stone and found a weight that suited her nicely. On the way, she inspired herself by piling up on the counter the weight in groceries that she had already lost. 'Just look at that, Ted,' she'd exclaim. 'Imagine carrying that extra weight around. It's quite ridiculous. I couldn't possibly lift it.'

Chapter 8: Brothers

When we arrived at Bromley, Jonathan was already part-way through his Maths degree at St John's College, Oxford. Patrick was finishing his studies at Bristol Grammar School before joining his brother there.

Mum and Dad were immensely proud of them both and especially of the Sir Thomas White Scholarship that Jonathan had won and of Patrick's Open Scholarship. In fact, we used to tease Mum that no one rang us up or came to the door without hearing all the details. Even a wrong number caller would be lucky to get away uninformed! I was keen to get in on the glory. When I first started primary school, the headmistress Mrs Long asked me what I wanted to do when I grew up. She was somewhat surprised to be told 'I want to go to St John's College, Oxford.'

Jonathan and Patrick were my heroes. Sweeping in for visits, one at a time, they brought laughter and fun in their wake. I'd never realised quite the effect these visits had on me until, on the eve of one of them arriving, a neighbour had looked at me in amazement. 'Christine, whatever is it? Your eyes are shining so and you're just bubbling over with joy!'

Their visits were packed with fun from the moment of their arrival. Often, as either of them unpacked, they'd find in their suitcase a doll in national costume eager to join my much-loved collection. Best of all, though, were the walks. Long, chatty walks along the lanes that I

Along Featherbed Lane

normally scurried along on my own in search of primroses and violets in spring and blackberries and elderberries in the autumn. I can especially remember Patrick and his girlfriend Laura teaching me how to skip like Morecombe and Wise down the very steep section of Featherbed Lane.

Exploring cross-country was always more problematic, as we often got halfway across a large field only to realise that we were being chased by a herd of bullocks who had been grazing unnoticed the far side of a hillock. Fear sprang strength into our legs as we thudded across the grassy tussocks and hurled ourselves over the five-bar gate, landing the other side doubled up in breathlessness with trembling knees and laughing with sheer relief.

Friends from Oxford were often brought home. A friend of Jonathan's who was a keen palaeontologist was thrilled to find a collection of ammonites in a local disused quarry. I had often found leaf fossils but these seemed huge and wonderful and I was delighted to be given some of the smaller ones to keep. I treasured them in an empty biscuit tin. The area was rich in geological interest, with seams of coal and quartz. In a nearby village, the local cobbler plied his trade from a cottage encrusted with pieces of quartz. I loved visiting there as a little girl, as it looked like something from a fairy tale. However, I must have felt a little too much at home, as Patrick recalls me greeting the elderly cobbler with a 'Good ... morning' punctuated by an enormous burp!

Brothers

Nempnett Thrubwell had such a pretty name that Patrick and I thought it would be a wonderful place to visit and imagined it full of thatched cottages and tearooms with roses round the door. An ice-cream van would be sure to stop there, to the delight of all the tourists, resting in the shade of chestnut trees on the village green. Many weary, winding lanes later we reached it. Not a village store in sight. No cosy village green with a park bench to sink down on. I began to moan for an ice cream. Just then my straggling feet, which had begun to scrape the toes from my shoes in protest, lost their grip on the uneven tarmac. I skidded across the road, skinning my knees and elbows. Patrick dabbed away with his handkerchief but there was blood dripping from several places at once. I was sobbing with tiredness as much as pain. No one was about. There were barely any houses anyway. Suddenly a car surprised us, coming round the corner into the village.

Startled out of my crying by the need for action, I took hold of Patrick's outstretched hand and we pressed ourselves against the hedgerow at the side of the road to give the car passing space. However, this was no ordinary driver. Instead of pushing past us and rumbling off into the distance, he wound down his window as he drew level with us and spoke to Patrick. 'Little un's in a sorry state, ain't she? You far from home?' When Patrick explained that we lived at Bromley Stores and that we had just been on a walk to explore Nempnett Thrubwell, the man

Along Featherbed Lane

chuckled. 'Bain't much to see, is there now? Would you two be wanting a ride home by any chance?' So it was that we drove home nestled in the cosy warmth of leather seats, catching our breath so that we were ready to tell our tale of adventure and rescue when we arrived home.

However, the most memorable incident was when Patrick, Laura and I went for a walk before Christmas dinner and got hopelessly lost. Eventually we tried taking a shortcut up a lane, which became muddier with each step. To our great relief, we eventually heard the sound of a tractor in the field ahead. Patrick went forward to ask the driver for directions. As the tractor turned for its next sweep of the field, we suddenly realised the job it was doing. Patrick was sprayed from head to toe in manure before the driver turned off his engine and told us the way home.

Chapter 9: Visiting Grandma

Generous as Jonathan and Patrick were, there was one request of mine which they never managed to fulfil. I always asked for a piggyback up the horribly steep St Michael's Hill in Clifton, Bristol but never really expected them to say yes. The enormous, breathless struggle to reach my Grandma's house in Tyndall's Park Road made such trips feel something of a pilgrimage.

Mum and Dad did not join us on these trips. However, Mum dutifully sent us off on the bus every now and again, burdened with the message, 'Joan sends her love,' to which we would receive the standard reply, 'And I send mine to her.'

Even when the immensely steep slope had been conquered, there was still the battle of the lift to win. Grandma's flat was at the top of a five-storey mansion.

The lift was small and select but entry to it required great strength or a perfectly acquired knack. Two heavy, arthritic metal doors had to be concertinaed back on themselves and then wrenched back into place before the journey could begin. Somehow the elderly residents managed this procedure but, given the choice, I always preferred the safety of the concrete stairs.

Once Grandma's door opened, we pushed our way past the heavy velvet door curtain into the flickering unreality of the fluorescent-lit hall. After the cosy chaos of Bromley Stores, these visits felt more like trips to a miniature stately home.

Along Featherbed Lane

The hall was large and imposingly gloomy. It was here that meals were served at the ample oak table, carefully covered with a green baize undercloth and a best lace cloth. This table stood against a bookcase of leather-bound sets of classics. Across the hall was a long expanse of sideboard, from which a rather pompous Toby jug and Toby teapot stared down at us. Every other room in the flat led off the hall and each door gave a pale shaft of light from the small fanlight above it. It was a place so hushed that even the air seemed trapped.

It was here that the first kiss of the visit had to be planted on Grandma's softly powdered waiting cheek. It was also here that a first glimpse of Auntie Elaine might be caught, standing quietly back. We were then asked to leave our coats on Grandma's bed, in a room almost as dark as the hall, since little light got past the thick brocade lace and velvet curtains. It was a splendid room of richest purples, blues and pinks, lavish with lace covers and fragrant with Houbigant perfume. On the dressing table Grandma's silver and pale blue satin brush and comb set was laid out. Everything was beautifully in its place.

From here we were invited to 'wash our hands' in the long, thin bathroom. The smell of gas from the aged water heater mingled with the stern cleanliness of coal tar or Pears soap. We were then allowed to enter the sunlit world of the lounge, where our feet sank into the deep pile Persian carpet with its delicate design of flowers. Rumoured to be the highest point in Bristol, the view

Visiting Grandma

from the long stretch of windows in this room was spectacular. The towers and turrets, rivers and bridges of the city were set out in miniature before us. Nearby were the imposing university buildings; in the distance the elegance of the Clifton Suspension Bridge.

The view inside the room was even more fascinating for me. Glass cabinets of fine ornaments and trinkets jostled with the bookcases to line the walls. There were no cosy sofas. Each person took up position in a stately armchair, with a small circular occasional table beside them on which to rest their teacup. Tea was soon brought in by Auntie Elaine on a wooden tea trolley that squeaked its way hesitantly through the carpet pile and around the low tables of glass and china ornaments.

Tea was served from a silver teapot, with a matching hot water jug used for making final adjustments of strength. White sugar lumps were chosen from the silver sugar bowl with the silver tongs. The patchwork tea cosy matched the scatter cushions which had been carefully worked in pastel pentagons of satin by Grandma.

Polite enquiries were made in every direction. The large ginger tom curled in sleep on a stool was admired. Like everything else though, he was not to be touched. A vicious temper and a delight in scratching out at strangers set this cat apart from the comfortable tabbies I had left at home. Presently Grandma grew weary of chatter and needed her afternoon rest. This was taken on the bed at the far end of the lounge, over which a beautiful cover was thrown during the day. Needing absolute darkness, Grandma first placed a navy silk scarf over her face and then covered this with the *Daily Telegraph*.

It was at this point, if I was visiting on my own, that Auntie Elaine would give me a beautiful smile framed with dark curls and beckon me away from the stillness. A gentle, thoughtful person, she well understood the specialness of childhood and the need for fun.

First we'd go exploring. Sometimes we'd go down the flights of fire escape stairs but usually we went up to the flat roof. This was Auntie Elaine's garden, which was decorated with tubs of flowers to be enjoyed from a canopied swing seat. Up here, in the fresh, heady air, she taught me to sing 'Kum Ba Yah' and 'The Mountains of Morne' and told me jokes. My favourite of these featured two brothers talking on the phone, when one of them had been away from home for a while.

'The first brother asked after his beloved cat.

"She's dead," said his brother.

"Don't just come out with it like that," he replied. "You should break it to me gently. Today you could have said that my cat was playing up on the roof. Then tomorrow you could have told me that she had fallen off and was at the vet's. Then the day after that you could have told me that she had passed away."

"Okay," his brother replied, "I get it."

The first brother then asked after their elderly mother.

Visiting Grandma

"Well," his brother answered, "today she's playing up on the roof...".'

After this we'd go down to Auntie Elaine's room, into which the daylight streamed. A jumbled assortment of well-thumbed orange Penguin classics and Critical Quarterly journals huddled together on wooden shelves over her desk. An assortment of mandolins, balalaikas and zithers were hung from the walls, whilst boxes of oddments for hobbies were half tucked away under her bed. However, even this refreshingly ordinary room had its mystery. Gazing at the walls long enough, I realised that a secret cupboard was set into a corner of the room, camouflaged with continuous wallpaper. Looking even more closely, I could see a tiny keyhole but no key.

All too soon, Grandma's rest was over and the state visit resumed. Afternoon tea was laid on the hall table. This was a dainty feast of finely sliced white bread and butter, shortbread and trifle. I drank weak, milky tea from a porcelain cup as carefully as I could. I remember on one visit being dressed in a Norwegian costume which had been bought for my Grandma when she was a little girl. I was very relieved that I managed to fit into it, as Grandma was anxious that a nice photo be taken of me wearing it.

I well remember the awful afternoon when I had been visiting on my own and we were joined for tea by an elderly couple. I managed to stay quiet and polite throughout the meal. Our guests gone, I enjoyed helping Auntie Elaine to clear the table. Clumsy with tiredness, I

Along Featherbed Lane

knocked the dregs from the gentleman's cup onto the tablecloth. I was absolutely terrified. Everything in that flat was perfect. With Auntie Elaine's blessing, I hid the stain under a tea plate and busied myself somewhere else. When Grandma came upon the stain, she must have quickly guessed what had happened and decided to give me the opportunity to confess my guilt. 'Well,' she exclaimed with cutting clarity, 'if Mr Taylor did that to my beautiful best tablecloth, he deserves to be told off. I shall ring him up immediately and demand an apology.' Even when she had the telephone in her hand and was pretending to dial, I stayed silent and felt sick.

Such drama was very rare though. The hours of our visits passed away in pleasantries. Both Grandma and Auntie Elaine were genuinely proud of our achievements at university and school and loved to hear details of them. In turn, they told us about their latest hobbies. Grandma enjoyed evening classes, took part in amateur dramatics and read to the blind. She was particularly fond of Dickens. Auntie Elaine's tales of herself were often seasoned with humour and always with modesty. She had a great desire to please people, even if this put her under enormous strain. The most extreme and comical example of this was when she treble-booked herself for one evening and tried to fulfil all three engagements. She accompanied Grandma to the theatre and then disappeared off to the 'toilet' for the first half of the play. Meanwhile, she returned to the flat to teach English to a group of young refugees. Having set them some work to

Visiting Grandma

finish, she managed to get to a concert being given by her dear friend Cynthia just in time to congratulate her during the interval. Then off to spend the play interval with Grandma and so on.

By now our visit to Grandma was nearly over, as time for the last bus to leave for home from the city centre was approaching. We lined up in the hall to place our farewell kiss on Grandma's cheek. Then away we flew hand in hand, stretching our legs, singing and laughing our way down St Michael's Hill.

Chapter 10: Mrs Long

After several years of being in Infants, the day came when I passed through the tall door into the Junior class. We would spend the rest of our time at Stanton Drew School in this classroom, moving year by year up the large year-group tables, away from the Infant class and towards the boiler.

This classroom was a place of awe and delight for me. All along the back of the classroom was a long shelf of books. Wonderful, exciting, challenging books, just waiting to be read. My favourites were the fat ones that had two books within the same cover. Once you had finished the first, you turned the book upside down and started on the second.

Above the books were a series of collage pictures worked in felt by former pupils, showing scenes of village life. Stretching high above these were the huge Victorian windows, set so far up in the wall that they could let in light but no distracting views. However, Mrs Long had peopled their sills with more wonderful examples of her pupils' needlework. Piglets and pincushion mice peeped over the edge, inspiring us in our sewing.

Sewing was the subject that was taken most seriously of all. Needlework classes were the only ones in which the pupils had to work in complete silence. At the end of the lesson any pupil who had spoken at all had to own up or be denounced by anyone who had heard them

Mrs Long

speak. Those who had managed to stay silent were rewarded with a coloured star, the lowest of those given for merit. Better still were silver and best of all were gold, given as a prize for only the most excellent effort or achievement. Within the hushed classroom, we were free to concentrate on perfecting our running stitches or tapestry.

I started out with a beige felt pincushion mouse. Once we had tacked a seam, we queued up in the long line waiting at Mrs Long's desk to have our work checked before moving on to sewing the seam itself. I was amazed to have my tacking criticised. 'No, Christine, even though these stitches are soon going to be taken out, they should be tiny and as neat as you can make them. As for the final stitches, they must be so perfect that you can scarcely see them at all. Then I'll be satisfied.' Mrs Long's instructions were always to be obeyed without question. I worked hard at making my stitches so tiny that they sank almost completely out of sight in the short pile of the felt.

Once the little mouse had been finished and taken home for Mum's delight and to fascinate Tiggy and Thomas, I was allowed to start on tapestry. Having been taught the basics, we were allowed to choose the colour of the wools and the design. I worked for months on a large square of canvas in shades of turquoise, yellow and peacock. I took care to keep it flat and not to pull hard on the thread, so that the finished surface of the tapestry would be level, with its furrows of wool running along evenly. Finally, when this was finished, I was allowed a similarly sized square of fine tan leather cloth to stitch behind the other, turning it into a hard-wearing knitting bag for Mum.

Everyone in the class was very proud of the lovely items we were helped to make. Mrs Long had the wonderful gift of encouragement. 'There's no such word as can't!' she would reply firmly if any of us started to flounder. Tall, with a powerful frame and an upright stance, Mrs Long exuded strength and confidence and inspired us to have self-confidence. The greatest testimony to this was the way that she taught us to swim. Way out in the countryside, with limited resources, she might easily have felt that even trying to find a way of teaching us to swim was beyond her. Not for Mrs Long.

A term's worth of weekly lessons was booked at a pool in Hotwells, Bristol and a coach hired. However, Mrs Long realised that much practice was going to be needed and that few of her children would be able to get the extra swimming required to gain the necessary confidence in the water. So, swimming training started way before we reached the pool. One afternoon we came into the classroom to find a bowl of water on her desk. Table by table we lined up to have a turn at holding our breath with our faces in the water. Then we were told to separate out our individual tables rather than having them clumped together into large year-group tables. We wondered what was coming next. We soon found out. We were told to lay across our tables facing the front of the

Mrs Long

classroom. Whilst we balanced on our tummies, our legs were free to learn the frog-like breaststroke movements over and over until they began to feel familiar. Finally, we were marched out into the playground for 'striding' practice. Taking large steps forward, we moved across the yard, doing the breaststroke action with our arms. Dipping our heads into the 'water' as our arms stretched straight out in front of us, we muttered 'bubble, bubble, bubble' until we came up for air as our arms fanned round to either side of us.

Finally the great day came to go to the swimming pool. We were allowed to take a few pennies with us to buy a treat from the chocolate machine after our lesson. Even the coach ride was a thrill. An elderly couple in a high-rise flat in Bristol waved to us and we all waved back enthusiastically. When we arrived, we hurried to get changed. There were swimming pool attendants there but Mrs Long stayed very much in charge of us. Still fully dressed herself, she directed us with absolute authority from the side of the pool. Those who were already strong swimmers went off to prove their ability to the attendant and to try out for different distances. The rest of us were lined up on one side of the pool and told to stride across, again and again, practising our arms and breathing just as we had in the playground. Week by week we did the same but in slightly deeper water each time. Gradually, one by one, our legs started to lift off the bottom of the pool and we were able to take off as fully fledged swimmers.

Along Featherbed Lane

Once we were confident swimming on our front, Mrs Long coached us one at a time to float on our backs. We started out by securing our toes firmly under the bar at the edge of the pool and then gingerly lying back in the water, firmly holding on to Mrs Long's thumb. As soon as we could do this whilst keeping our stomachs high in the water, the instruction came to let go of her thumb. We were used to doing as we were told, so soon we were all truly afloat. After this we had fun practising our widths week by week until, as we gained in strength and confidence, we were taken up to the deep end to try out for a whole length on our own. With aching limbs and shining eyes, we bought our little boxes of Poppets for the return trip and sank deeply back in our seats to compare notes with our friends. Nancy was an excellent swimmer, so spent her time at the deep end. It was fun to hear of her dives and long swims and she encouraged me about my widths and eventual length.

Another great strength of Mrs Long's was her coaching of us in French conversation. Educated herself at the Sorbonne, she took much delight in sharing her love of the French language with us. As well as learning how to speak many basic phrases, we took pride in our ability to sing French songs. When there was a Junior Schools' get-together at the Chew Valley School, the local Secondary School, it was no surprise that our party piece for the closing concert was a French round 'Vent frais, vent du matin', which rang out sweetly and strongly from our small school group.

Mrs Long

Nancy and I were paired up for French conversation. We were all given French names, written out on cardboard plaques and worn around our necks. These names were based wherever possible on French versions of our first or middle names. In this way Nancy and I became Virginie and Marie one afternoon a week. Our conversation remained the same but grew in confidence, as each week we all had to perform it to the rest of the class. After exchanging greetings and asking 'Ça va?' of one another, we then progressed to checking the time and, on hearing how late it was, the glorious climax 'Zut alors! Au revoir Virginie. A bientôt!'

I held Mrs Long in such high esteem that on occasion Mum attempted to use her influence to good effect on some wayward aspect of my behaviour. When I had exclaimed that 'the bloody cat has gone upstairs again', Mum gently chided, 'Now, Christine, what would happen if Mrs Long heard you saying that?' After a few moments' thought came my puzzled reply 'But we don't have a cat at school.'

Our education was deeply rooted in village life. Visiting the prehistoric Stanton stone circles was given special significance by Mrs Long, who told us the village tale of how they came about. The local sweethearts Kitty Stanton and Johnny Drew loved dancing so much that, after their wedding, they partied late into the night. When midnight approached, the village musicians packed up their instruments as Sabbath law dictated, much to Kitty and Johnny's disappointment. Just then a stranger

Along Featherbed Lane

appeared with a fiddle and offered to play for them as long as they wished. They agreed but, as they danced past midnight, the fiddler threw back his cloak to reveal himself as the devil and the wedding guests were turned into stones. They can still be seen to this day, standing in their dancing circles.

The reality of visiting the stones was a little less shrouded in myth and mystery. The farmer who owned the field in which they stood seemed rather to begrudge having a tourist attraction on his property. He had encircled them with electric fencing and grazing cattle. It was a great concession that he turned off the current so that we could approach the stones, where they hunched over or lay fallen in the long straggling grasses. It was a very hot afternoon and the walk back to school was wearisome, as we gasped the dry, pollen-laden air past our parched lips.

'Mrs Long, can we have a drink of water when we get in, please Miss?' we pleaded.

'Yes, of course you can, as long as you queue nicely by the water fountain for your turn. Mind you, children, can you guess which drink would refresh you more on a day like this—iced lemonade or a good, hot cup of tea?'

'The lemonade,' we all chorused thirstily.

'No, children, you're wrong. If I had that choice I would go for the tea, which would make me perspire and cool me down beautifully.' This logic was beyond us. For

Mrs Long

once, we wondered if the heat might possibly be affecting Mrs Long just as badly as it was us.

Every year, in the autumn, Mrs Long handed each of us a wrinkly brown bulb to take home. 'Take care of these, children. Go home and plant them deeply in the ground. Then mark the spot with four sticks pushed in to form a square around the bulb. We'll leave them to sleep for a while but, come the spring ... well, just you wait and see!'

Spring came in gently after the cruelty of winter. The little frozen waterfalls, poised at the sides of Featherbed Lane where the rainwater trying to escape the surrounding fields had been held in silent captivity for weeks, now started to drip. Celandines and violets peeped out from the banks.

Soon came the instruction, 'It's time, children, to go and look at the place where you've buried your bulb.' Almost forgotten, it was fun to visit the spot again. There, pushing its way through the light overlay of weeds was a pale green tip straining towards the light. We all crowded round Mrs Long's desk the following morning, talking at once. 'Come on everyone, sit down and I'll tell you your task for today. You are to find a good-sized flowerpot, sturdy, strong and with no cracks in it. Then very, very carefully, you are to dig up your daffodil and make it at home in the pot, with plenty of soil pressed down firmly enough to make it feel snug and secure. Then bring it into school tomorrow, along with an old plate that your mothers give you to rest it on.'

Along Featherbed Lane

Our daffodils proudly lined the window ledges for weeks. Each pot was labelled with our name, as the plants were equally strong and beautiful. All, that is, except mine. The three previous years I had grown beautiful daffodils like everyone else. I had hoped, like everyone else, that mine would be chosen as one of the best three and receive a prize. I had been disappointed, like so many others. This year was going to be different. It had to be. It was my last chance.

The ground was harder than it looked and, as I tried to dig the bulb up this year, the spade skidded over the surface and sliced off the very tip of my daffodil. Numb with horror, I quickly dug it up, pushed it into its waiting pot and ran into the house to tell Mum. She listened kindly but did not share my despair.

'It's all right, Chrissie, dear. There are plenty of daffodils pushing their way through in the garden just now. You can take one of those instead.'

'No, no, no I can't!' I shouted, stamping my feet. 'Don't you understand? This was the bulb I was given to look after. This is the bulb Mrs Long gave me. No matter what it looks like, this is my daffodil.'

I expected a scolding when I took it into school the following day but it did not come. One look at my stricken face was probably enough for Mrs Long. 'Don't worry so, Christine. You'll be surprised at how beautiful it can still be.'

Such encouragement was needed as many long hours were spent with our daffodils over the next few

Mrs Long

weeks. We measured them, practising those newfangled centimetres. We watered and turned them, lined up in pride of place along the window ledges. We drew pictures of them every week. We wrote descriptions of them in loving detail. And I did begin to love my daffodil. It seemed determined to flourish, despite its poor start. Leaves lengthened, buds burgeoned, swelling imperceptibly in front of my eager eyes. Three flowers unfurled and trumpeted their glory. It was the most beautiful daffodil I had grown by far.

The day had come at last. Mr Guard, a Rural Science teacher from Chew Valley School, came to admire our daffodils and select the finest. I had given up all hope of prizes. However, I was very proud of my daffodil and hoped he wouldn't mark me out for criticism for the damaged leaf ends.

Accompanied by Mrs Long, Mr Guard threaded his way between our tables with his notebook. Round and round he went, carefully observing every detail of our plants, whilst out of the corner of our eyes we observed him. Every nod, smile or frown was noted. When he passed my daffodil for the second time, I spotted Mrs Long say something to him. On he went, checking and making notes.

Eventually Mrs Long stood behind her desk, with Mr Guard smiling besides her. 'Well, children, you have done well again this year. These are all really beautiful daffodils. Well done all of you. Mrs Long has asked me to select the three finest daffodils and it has been a

Along Featherbed Lane

difficult task...'. Out of her desk, Mrs Long brought a white paper bag with some crisp, new Ladybird books in it, which she spread across her table. 'In first place...'. My mind was daydreaming, wondering what the books were. I scarcely noticed who had won and automatically joined in the clapping. 'In second place...'. Suddenly Nancy was nudging me hard and the other children were turning round to look at me. I realised that he had just called out my name. Clutching my prize so tightly that my knuckles turned white, I glanced at Mrs Long and received a beaming smile.

Chapter 11: Stormy weather

As much as I enjoyed school now, there was one subject that I still dreaded. One afternoon a week, we stepped down from the sunlit playground into the lane outside and filed in our pairs to the right. There were no pavements. We plunged down to where the trees knit their fingers over the road. Shafts of light feebly tried to penetrate the emerald gloom. We huddled close to the steep bank on our side of the road. Among the long, straggling grasses were the long tongued leaves and temptingly red berry cones of 'lords and ladies', too poisonous to touch. Even on a hot day this overshadowed stretch of lane was cold. We shivered with our bare arms and legs.

Suddenly stopped by Mrs Long, we carefully looked right and left and right again before crossing. All too soon came a stile, set up on the opposite bank. Slowly, carefully, we clambered over the stile one at a time and tumbled out onto the school playing field.

An overweight and asthmatic child, I loathed these afternoons of breathless races and trembling legs. The only redeeming feature was sitting on the grass with my friends Nancy and Pat, chatting and threading daisy chains in between races. Egg and spoon was my best chance at not coming in last but I hated the sack race, skipping race and flat race with a vengeance.

One Tuesday evening, knowing that the following afternoon was going to be sports day if the weather was good, I decided to try a different approach. I was used to praying for Mum, Dad and my brothers. This time I added on an extra, silent prayer. 'Please, God, make it rain tomorrow, especially in the afternoon. Amen.'

Wednesday 10th July 1968 dawned much like any other day. There was a difference, though. We had a parents' evening at school and Mum had agreed to come along. Our next door neighbour Mrs Cole had kindly offered to give us a lift there at 7 pm.

By lunchtime the summer sky began to darken and the classroom seemed gloomy. Instead of birdsong, we heard the pattering of rain: heavy, drenching rain. Mrs Long was not easily moved from her plans. However, on this particular afternoon she decided that we should tidy the classroom and lay out our best pieces of work on our desks rather than going to the playing field. I was overjoyed. Lovingly, I placed book after book of precious stories and poems open on my desk, as well as some of my favourite pictures. I loved my firework picture, scratched out of the top layer of black wax crayon with a darning needle to reveal the beautiful carnival of colours wax crayoned underneath. I couldn't wait to show Mum.

The rain had done its job well but it didn't know when to stop. The odd rumble of thunder cracked the stillness of the end of the school day and one of the lads shot under Mrs Long's table well, refusing to come out. Mrs Long tried everything from kindly coaxing to stern ordering but nothing would uncurl the boy huddling at

Stormy weather

her feet. Thankfully the school day soon ended and he had to come out to be collected by his mum.

When I got home, I was greeted by the random patter of drips of rain falling into a collection of buckets and bowls all along the seam where the shop had been added onto the front of the house. There was nothing unusual about this. It always leaked when the rain blew in from a certain angle. Today, though, it seemed to be pouring constantly from every angle. Mum greeted me with 'Chrissie, dear, will you just pop upstairs and see if any of the bedroom ceilings are leaking. I'll bet they are, somewhere or other. Just take these ice-cream tubs up and try to catch them before they leak through, will you? Use this old newspaper to sog up any puddles. All the proper buckets and bowls are already in use down here.' Sure enough, I found several damp patches on the carpet and I carefully positioned the tubs until several drips had landed centrally in each. Most of the newspaper I put underneath to soak up some of the water but I saved a little to put in the base of each tub so that the drip didn't bounce off the plastic so hard that some of it landed outside the tub anyway.

We soon sat down to tea and I told Mum over and over all the different things I wanted her to look at. I envisaged my way around the classroom describing all the books, pictures and window ledge handicrafts that were favourites of mine and that I wanted to share with her. Then I went through in detail for both Mum and Dad all the work I had on display, so that Mum knew what to

Along Featherbed Lane

look out for and Dad could imagine it all and participate in this way. Whilst Mum washed up the dishes and tidied her hair, I went round the shop and house emptying any of the containers that were filling fast.

It should have been a gentle summer evening but instead it was black as night.

'The forecast isn't good, Joan,' my Dad warned. 'Are you sure you should be going out in it?'

'Of course I am, Ted. I've been looking forward to this for weeks. Anyway, if there was a problem Mrs Long would have cancelled it and rung us up by now.'

'Well, at least make sure you've both got some good footwear on and macs and scarves. Either of you can borrow my monsoon cape if you want, you do know that.' We all started laughing at this. Dad had a huge, dusty khaki monsoon cape from when he was stationed in the Burmese jungle during the Second World War. He insisted on keeping it on hand as a viable option for rainy days. In reality, the only ones who found it desirable were the emaciated spiders that hid in its deep folds.

However, when seven o'clock came and we went out of the shop door to get into Mrs Cole's car, we were in for a shock. Sheets of rain were hurtling down into the darkness and making it desperately hard for her to see out of her windscreen. Streams of black water were running swiftly down either side of the road. Mum and Mrs Cole chatted all the way to the school about how they couldn't remember such a hard rainstorm and how, after so many hours of rain, it must be due to stop soon.

Stormy weather

Apart from getting my feet very wet in the few steps between the car and the school, I was uninterested in the weather. I wanted Mum to be dazzled by the wonderful place in which I spent my days. During my time in the Infants, the contact between school and home had been very uncomfortable. Even when our strike to gain a school taxi was over, I was not popular with the teacher. Between bouts of asthma and crippling stomach pains caused by my egg allergy, I often missed a day of school and the inspector was frequently sent round to check on the reasons for my poor attendance.

Today was the beginning of something new. Mrs Long spoke kindly of me and my work to Mum. However, as the evening drew on she began to look very tired and anxious. Mum's hope of having a longer chat with her seemed unlikely, even though we hovered close by waiting for an opportunity. Suddenly, Mrs Cole was at Mum's side, 'Sorry about this, Mrs Longhurst, but I really think we should be getting back home now. Believe it or not, the weather looks worse now rather than better.' Reluctantly, we followed her through deepening puddles to her car. Sure enough, the rain was like a heavy curtain falling around us. Just as we set off, forks of lightning hurtled down a few fields away, followed almost immediately by thunder tearing the air apart. None of us could get home fast enough. It felt as if we were being chased by a monstrous black dog, howling in deep-bellied fury and slashing down at us with his fangs.

Along Featherbed Lane

Dad was white-faced when we bundled into the shop, dripping and talking both at once. 'Seriously, Joan, I've never seen weather quite like this. The pressure is all over the place. I keep tapping the barometer just to see what's going to happen next and I can feel the change in my forehead.' After hot milky drinks and a last tour of the buckets to empty the water away before the night, I snuggled into bed. Thunder and lightning notwithstanding, I was exhausted with all the excitement of the day.

I woke up to a shock. 'No need to rush up this morning, Tina Mary,' my Dad called out. 'There will definitely be no school today. If you want to see why, go and look out of the front bedroom window.' Curious at this strange news, I opened the red floral curtains and gasped. Not only had the road turned into a stream but huge swathes of the fields around us were lakes. No cars passed. 'There was one poor soul, late last night,' Dad told me, 'who asked if we knew which roads were open for him to take back to Bristol. He said he'd been driving round and round but it felt as if this stretch of roads was now an island. I asked if he wanted to stay here for the night but he was determined to get home if he could before it got any worse. Hope he made it all right.'

Dad listened to the radio reports and Mum chatted away to anyone who reached our shop, gleaning the local reports.

'Over five inches of rain, all in one day. No wonder the streams burst their banks,' Dad reflected.

Stormy weather

'It was more than a few burst banks,' Mum replied. 'Apparently, the bridge at Pensford was destroyed and conditions at Chew Magna sound just terrible. I've never seen anything like it. Geoff was saying that by the time it reached Keynsham, it was a ten foot tall tidal wave.'

Just then the phone rang and Dad answered. We wondered who he was talking to for so long, describing what had happened and how close the flood water was to us now. 'Well, Joan,' he said once he had put down the receiver, 'I had no idea how lucky we'd been in all of this. Apparently, most of the local phones are down. That chap has been ringing round to see if he could find any local ones still working. Mustn't take the electricity for granted either. A lot of poor souls have been cut off. Imagine making it through last night in the pitch black. It doesn't bear thinking.'

Gradually, the water ebbed away and the customers returned, each bringing their tale of what happened to them on the night of the 'Great Flood of 1968' as it came to be known. It turned out that Mrs Long had very real reason to be growing anxious as the rain fell that evening. Her daughter was left alone in their riverside home. The water rose so fast that she was eventually rescued by firemen in a boat from her bedroom window. Other people had to climb up into their attics to cheat the rising flood. Bridges were swept away, some with people still on them.

Aged seven and a half, most of the facts and figures passed over my head. However, the story about

Along Featherbed Lane

Mrs Long's daughter troubled me and I kept imagining how terrifying it would have been to have the dark, angry water occupying the ground floor and creeping after you up the stairs. With a sudden jolt, I remembered something I'd forgotten in all the terror and excitement. I had prayed for rain and look what had happened. I felt hollow-stomached with guilt. This was one secret I couldn't keep to myself. I ran to find Mum but when I'd found her I didn't know how to begin. 'Whatever is it, Chrissie? You look as white as a sheet!' Slowly, staring hard at my scuffed shoes as I spoke, I explained about how much I hated sport afternoons and about my prayer, about how sorry I was that it had rained too much and caused so many problems.

I was interrupted by what sounded like a stifled giggle. Glancing at Mum, I saw that she was holding a large handkerchief over her mouth and nose. When she met my puzzled gaze she quickly blew her nose. 'Well, Christine, I think you've learned your lesson. You shouldn't pray selfish prayers, like asking for rain to spoil the sports afternoon that everyone else enjoys so much. Still, I'm quite sure that God doesn't want you to feel responsible for the flood. That was His idea, not yours. Now stop worrying and give me a hand with laying the table for tea.' Reassured, I set off to the kitchen with a skip in my step and a lighter heart.

We may have escaped the flood with nothing but a few more yellow-edged stains on the ceilings, where the rain had leaked through that night, but the weather

Stormy weather

at Bromley was often challenging and sometimes dangerous. It seemed as if this area was often on the divide between different weather systems. This meant that at times the weather at the front and back of our house could be radically different. The most memorable example of this was when the shop was bathed in warm, summer sunshine. However, when I tried to go out of the back door to play on my swing, I was pushed back by hundreds of tiny stabbing fingers of hail, which piled up in drifts, white on the ground. These hailstones were like small marbles, mercilessly stinging any bare arms and legs they could reach.

At least the hail soon melted away. Other attacks by the weather were more savage and permanent. Every spell of sultry summer weather seemed to be chased off by a violent thunderstorm. We would count the interval between the lightning strike and the thunderclap to see how close the storm was. One second per mile, Dad would say. All too often, there was barely time to start counting before the air shuddered with the force of the thunder. If the count was under three, Dad would unplug the television and Mum wouldn't use the telephone until the storm had passed. These precautions were unsurprising since, in our early days at Bromley, both the telephone line and our television aerial had been struck by lightning. Moreover, the beautiful, double white lilac, under which we used to sit and play with the cats, was blasted and encircled with a sterile deadness in the soil in which nothing could flourish.

Along Featherbed Lane

Once the summer storms died down, the autumn gales had their turn. In the later years of our living at Bromley, there was one particularly savage night of creakings and howls. When we ventured out the next morning the whole garden looked battered and bewildered. Then we saw it. Our biggest apple tree, under which we had picnicked so often, had been ripped up. It was leaning over at 45 degrees, its roots clawing pitifully in the air for support. My swing was left dangling lopsidedly fifteen feet up in the air.

Chapter 12: Going to church

Few of the parents of children at my school came to our shop. One exception was Mrs Hope-Simpson, who had a daughter at Stanton Drew School a few years younger than me. She pleasantly surprised us one day by asking Mum if I'd like to join the church choir. St Mary's was at the top of a hill on the far side of the village. Jonathan had taken me to services there sometimes on his visits home and I had been to a Methodist church a few times when I'd stayed with Grandma and Auntie Elaine and quite enjoyed it. More than anything else, I loved singing, so this invitation was irresistible. From then on, every Friday evening and Sunday morning and evening, Mrs Hope-Simpson, who turned out to be the organist as well as our customer, kindly gave me a lift to the church with her daughter Vicky.

I felt very nervous about going to the first choir practice. I wondered who would be there and if they'd welcome me. I didn't need to worry. Following close on the heels of Mrs Hope-Simpson and Vicky, I slipped quietly into the church. Pat, a girl of my own age, rushed up to me, 'Oh, Christine, you've come after all. That's great. We could do with you helping to sing the tune.' Lowering her voice and peeping over her shoulder at the elderly man humming his way loudly through the hymn book, she confided, 'Otherwise all they can hear is the tenor line.' Pat grabbed me by the arm and took charge of me. She was the vicar's eldest child and had been a good

Along Featherbed Lane

friend at Stanton Drew School. However, she had been sent to Clifton High in Bristol instead. I had missed her.

It turned out that we were the two oldest of the six children in the choir. Mr Brown was the only man. A relation of Mrs Tovey, he was already a familiar, kindly face. Apart from Mrs Hope-Simpson, the only lady was the assistant organist Liz, the big sister of a boy from Stanton Drew School. With the ladies busy playing the organ, Pat and I often had the challenge of keeping the tune going. Not only did we sing hymns but also psalms, responses and all the traditional chants for the 'Jubilate', 'Nunc Dimittis', 'Te Deum' and so on, as well as practising hard the descant for 'The Lord's my Shepherd', to the tune 'Crimond'. We sang our hearts out and so did Mr Brown. Finally, one day Mrs Brown said to me after the service. 'Well, Christine, I could really hear you singing today.' I remember not knowing whether to feel chuffed or annoyed that all my singing over the previous months had been inaudible!

Pat's father, Revd Russell, was a vicar who displayed amazing patience and perseverance in caring for his flock. Working part-time as a teacher to supplement his parish income, he tried week in and week out to encourage us in our giving. Week in and week out, the congregation listened politely enough and then dropped their odd pennies into the collection plate.

Revd Russell was a dedicated visiting vicar. This was not always appreciated by the people who lived in his parish. Some of our neighbours were known to pass on

Going to church

the word that 'Vicar's on his way!' before turning off their lights and laying low when he rang on their bell.

Mum, however, always gave him a warm welcome, bringing out a plate of our latest batch of cakes. Chocolate caramel slices were especially popular and to some extent made up for the fact that Dad wasn't well enough to stay awake for long, even when we had visitors. So whilst Dad snored gently in the corner, Mum would hear the latest news of parish life and have a welcome chance to share her worries about my Dad's health. They were also able to tell each other how well Pat and I were doing at school.

Revd Russell liked to support Jonathan in his teaching career, always adding in a special prayer for schoolteachers when he came to church on a visit home. A great encourager of others, it must have been a hard parish in which to keep his enthusiasm. Like so many of the parishioners, the fabric of the church was elderly and frail. Once, when Jonathan leaned his elbows on the bookrest in front of him as he knelt to pray, a whole section of rotten wood broke off. Jonathan handed in the large chunk of wooden pew with an apology when he shook Revd Russell's hand at the end of the service and the vicar made light of it.

One day when Revd Russell visited, he had an air of excitement about him. When Mum offered to put on the kettle, he stopped her. 'That's very kind, Mrs Longhurst, but actually today I'm here for a special reason. I'd especially like you to stay and hear what I

Along Featherbed Lane

have to say. Christine has been a loyal member of our choir now for months, hasn't she? Now, I don't know if you knew this, but the Bishop is coming to St Mary's in a fortnight to confirm some of our young people. I don't know why it didn't cross my mind to ask her before but I was wondering if Christine would like to be confirmed too. It strikes me quite strongly that she is a dedicated member of our church and should be given this opportunity.'

For once, we were all taken aback. I had no idea what being confirmed was and wondered what it was that I was being asked to do. I'm not sure what Dad was thinking but he was certainly wide awake. Mum was puzzled about the practicalities.

'That's lovely of you to think of including Christine in your confirmation group but surely she would need to go to classes?'

'Don't worry about that,' Revd Russell responded cheerfully, 'I have been giving the matter some thought. Of course, I have been taking classes with the other candidates for some time now and we have been studying this book.' With that, he opened his briefcase and produced a little prayer book and catechism designed for use with youngsters preparing for confirmation. He handed it to me. 'If you decide that you would like to be confirmed, Christine, I will need you to study this book and to learn the Apostle's Creed. Maybe you and your mum could look at the catechism together. Then, on Wednesday evening at seven o'clock, you will need to

Going to church

join the rest of the candidates in the vicarage for last-minute preparation and to make sure that everyone understands what they need to say and do on the day. Have a think about it and then perhaps your mum would kindly give me a ring if you want to join in. If you do decide to, then your mum will need to have a word with my wife about suitable clothing for you for the service. Anyway, please have a look at the book and have a good think about it.'

So it was that, a fortnight later, I was helping Mum up the hill to St Mary's Church. My godmother Vera was on the other side of Mum, holding her arm and offering encouragement. Mum had been very busy in the interim, having been lent a paper pattern for a suitable confirmation dress by the vicar's wife. It was a high necked dress with full-length puffed sleeves with strips of the material sewn onto either side and tied in a bow at the back. Made in white crimplene, which fell in soft folds to several inches below the knee, it was a very simple, lovely dress. When we arrived, I was whisked to one side along with the other girls being confirmed, including Pat and Nancy. We then had large folded squares of plain white cotton fastened to the front of our hair with hair grips, as veils. Bishop Edward of Bath and Wells seemed a tall, imposing figure as we knelt on the cushioned rail in front of him and answered his questions. He then moved along the row of waiting children, placing his hand on each head in turn. I firmly re-pinned my veil, which kept trying to slip off backwards. My faith then was mostly

Along Featherbed Lane

an attitude of heart rather than one based on an understanding of Scripture. Still, I felt in that blessing a tremendous warmth of belonging. After the service, the bishop became a gentle, kindly figure who signed our prayer books.

It had been a shiningly wonderful evening but all too soon we were winding our way back down the hill and kissing Vera goodbye. Vera had been my Mum's best friend since they were at kindergarten together. Several times a year, Vera would drive us to her home in Fishponds, Bristol for afternoon tea. She had a lovely garden with a large lawn for playing with her dogs. I was a little afraid of dogs, as in the country they were usually large and fierce, mostly Alsatians. Vera's dogs were different. She loved them like children and brought them up to behave well. There were silky ears to stroke and rough tummies to tickle without fear of being nipped.

Mum loved having a tour of the garden, admiring Vera's plants and being given some of the latest crop of tomatoes or runner beans to take home. At the end of the afternoon, we went into the dining room. In the bay window overlooking the garden a table was set, laden with delights. Cucumber sandwiches and cheese sandwiches cut into small triangles, sausage rolls, peanuts in glass dishes, sliced beetroot, homemade chutney, shortbread, fruit cake and, my favourite of all, a plate starry with iced gem biscuits. As soon as we had finished, Mum would offer to help wash up but Vera would refuse. 'That's nice of you to offer, Joan, but I want today to be a

Going to church

treat. You can wash up all the other days when you're home. Speaking of which, I'd better be taking you back before Ted wonders what's happened to you. It's such a shame that he's not strong enough to come himself these days.' Mum agreed but said how much he would enjoy the beautiful tomatoes that Vera had given us. I loved those visits but I also loved going home, recognising the familiar hills and trees as we threaded our way through the winding lanes, which were richly lined with blackberries and dangling bunches of elderberries.

Chapter 13: Moving on

At Bromley we ate according to season, enjoying strawberries on summer evenings, apples, pears and pumpkins in the autumn and shaking the winter snow off our Brussels sprouts. Spring was my favourite time of year, though, when the harvest was of daily posies of primroses and violets and the house martins came home to nest in our roof.

It felt as if life would go on the same forever, with the seasons weaving in and out of each other's way like maypole dancers. Still, change was on its way. Within two months of each other, both Patrick and Laura and Jonathan and Judith got married. Patrick and Laura's wedding was mellow with autumn and rich with satin and lace in a country church full of flowers. Jonathan and Judith's wedding was winter elegance of white and blue velvet in the London church at which Judith had grown up. Jonathan and Judith settled in St Albans, from where they both worked as secondary school teachers. Patrick and Laura went to London, where Patrick trained as an actuary and Laura worked as a nurse and trained to be a health visitor.

After several years of teaching in England, Jonathan and Judith decided to spend a few years working in Ghana. Saying goodbye for so long was very hard. However, the weekly letters soon started to arrive and Mum, Dad and I began to enjoy the adventure of Jonathan and Judith's life in Ghana vicariously. Tales of

Moving on

flying fish seen from the ship in which they sailed to Ghana set the pace. From then on we heard wonderful accounts of plunging down the unimaginable depths of a gold mine, of tiny gecko lizards scampering up the walls, of a huge spider found under their bed and of a monstrously long monitor lizard hurtling through their garden. Our imaginations were warmed with tropical sunshine and brilliantly coloured costumes, fruits and creatures.

Mum delighted in passing on snippets of these accounts to favoured customers. I used them to give an illustrated talk at school. Mrs Long was so delighted that she awarded me 100%.

However, even for me times were changing. I had reached the end of my time at Stanton Drew School. This was doubly sad for me. Not only would I miss Mrs Long and all her wisdom and encouragement but Nancy told me that she was going to go to the local convent school rather than to Chew Valley School. We promised to keep in touch and we have, to this day. Still, those goodbyes were painful. Our final day at school ended, as all the others had, in prayer, with each of us standing beside our desks onto which we had lifted our chairs. 'As the shadows lengthen, the busy world is hushed, the fever of life is over and our work done, Lord, in your mercy, grant us safe lodging, a holy rest and peace at the last. Amen.' Those words had flooded our weary minds and bodies with peace each day, quietening the bustle in and around

Along Featherbed Lane

us and sending us home restored. Our days at the school had started with a hymn. Of these, my favourite was:

> Little drops of water,
> Little grains of sand,
> Make the mighty ocean
> And the beauteous land.
>
> Little deeds of kindness,
> Little words of love,
> Make this earth an Eden,
> Like the Heaven above.

    Mrs Long had taught us well how much the little things in this life count. She had taken the time and trouble to visit the elderly couple who always waved to us so enthusiastically from their top-floor council flat when we drove past on our way to swimming lessons. She had discovered that they had a golden wedding coming up the following week. That Wednesday we were all told to bring to school the next day the prettiest bunch of flowers from our garden that we could manage as a gift for them. Mum gave me a bunch of sweet-smelling white phlox to take. Everyone in the class had remembered and took pleasure in showing Mrs Long the bunches that they had carefully clutched all the way to school. Between us, we had brought bucketfuls of the most gorgeous flowers to brighten that kind couple's flat.

Chapter 14: Chew Valley School

Autumn came shrouded in mist to our valley. Looking out for the school coach to take me to my secondary school was a case of peering through the tiny window behind the counter, over Mrs Tovey's front garden with the shrubs decked out in spiders' webs sparkling with dew. The swirling fog reduced visibility so much that it was only when the school bus reached halfway down our road that it suddenly lurched into sight, cream against the whiteness. Box-like, with a wooden interior, this was a coach that had more of a past than a future and no discernible suspension. It was nicknamed the 'boneshaker'.

Hunched over my large leather satchel, I ducked onto the nearest free seat, second row from the front on the driver's side. I hugged my satchel firmly on my lap and, once we had started moving again, stole a glance at the children around me. So far, so good. No one seemed loud or bullying. The girls in front of me both had nut brown hair: one short and neat and the other carefully parted down the middle into two bunches, which were held out from each side of her head by green plastic bobbles on elastic. The bobbles impressed me. They were just the right colour for our school uniform, bottle green. Just about everything else was already matching: bottle green blazer, bottle green jumper, bottle green socks and even bottle green knickers. The only relief was a grey skirt and white shirt with a tie striped with green and red.

Along Featherbed Lane

I missed the prettier blue of my old school jumper and the white lacy socks. My daydreams about Stanton Drew School were suddenly interrupted. The short-haired girl turned and looked over her shoulder at me with a smile.

'I'm Jane. You're a First Year, aren't you? Just like my little sister Claire here.' Claire, the girl with the bobbles, frowned a bit at this but Jane continued cheerfully, 'Fine sort of a little sister she is, already a good two inches taller than me. Still, as far as I'm concerned, she's my little sister and always will be.'

Claire was now looking over her shoulder too. 'Wish I knew which class I was going to be in. Jane's been telling me all about the First Year form teachers. Half of them sound mad and the rest don't sound much better. It would have been good to have found out before the summer so that we had the chance to prepare ourselves.'

I had expected just to listen to them chatting away but now curiosity got the better of me. 'Please would you tell me what they're like? I don't really know anything about the school,' I admitted. Jane needed no further encouragement but set about telling me all about the school with such kindness and good humour that I began to feel at my ease. Claire would chip in as often as she could with the bits of information she already knew, so that the conversation batted back and forth easily between them.

By the time that they had finished talking, we were almost out of Stanton Drew. I spotted Nancy and her

Chew Valley School

older sister walking to the convent school in Chew Magna. She suddenly looked very grown-up and smart. I wished so much that she was coming to Chew Valley School with me. They glanced up as the coach swung past them and I waved, just in case Nancy could see me. When they were out of sight, I slumped back down into my seat and folded my arms even more tightly around my satchel. The coach then wound its way left past The Round House, a tiny thatched cottage set in the middle of the T-junction where the road from Stanton Drew joined the busier road going to Chew Magna. Set in a little triangle of grass, this property had once been a toll house. It always fascinated me. Spick and span, with clean windows, a mowed lawn and white exterior, it was obviously lived in and loved. However, in all the years that I went past it, I never spotted the owner.

Soon after this we plunged into the shadiness of deep-cut walls. The coach wove its way carefully, needing to sway to one side almost to scraping point in order to let approaching vehicles pass. Eventually, we soared back into the softness of sunlit hedgerows. Skirting the tiny cricket pitch, we arrived at Chew Magna. With its raised, railed pavements and proper high street of shops, Chew Magna was a place of wonder. It had everything: a bank, an estate agent's, a doctors' surgery, a vet and, at times, a dentist. There was a shop that sold school uniforms and sports equipment and a Post Office that sold beautiful birthday cards and luxurious beauty products, such as presentation boxes of

Along Featherbed Lane

Bronnley soap and Mum's favourite, 4711 cologne sticks. There was even a choice of two grocery stores, including a very small branch of the Co-op. I tried to ignore the butcher's, with a large carcass hanging upside down in the doorway, ready for jointing. Apart from that, I gazed eagerly at the shops we passed, enjoying the window displays and hanging baskets.

    All too soon we left Chew Magna behind and turned left up the road to my new school. Green fields edged with swirling mists stretched away on either side of the road. As we reached the school it looked as though a groundsman had been sweeping back the mist to reveal the whole school and its playing fields in their dew-washed glory. Shafts of sunlight were peeping over the distant hedgerows and fanning the fields. Weary from being rattled on the wooden seats, we stretched our legs and stepped gingerly down the steep coach steps onto the sunny playground. I decided there and then that it would be a good idea to follow Claire. This was a good decision.

Chapter 15: A new friend

To my delight, Claire was put in the same form as me. However, she sat in the row in front of me with friends from her primary school. I was seated in the back row with several girls from Stanton Drew. It was reassuring to be able to chat to girls I knew, even if they were not special friends.

Our form room was the newly installed language laboratory. Each desk had a set of headphones and a microphone. The teacher had a master control panel that meant that he could select one pupil to listen to at a time and privately make his comment to them on their accent, even though we were all talking at once. After Mrs Long's coaching in French conversation, speaking in French held no fears for us. Nevertheless, it was still a bit intimidating when you heard a silencing of background hum and realised that you were the one being listened to. Our form teacher was a big, bearded bear of a man who encouraged excellence but did not spare the sarcasm if anything fell below his expected standards.

I was determined not to attract his sarcasm and all went well. I was even more determined not to be bullied. One lad tried his luck by jeering at me as he handed out dictionaries and giving me one with a broken spine and missing pages. Something broke in me as I recognised the sickly fear growing in the pit of my stomach. 'Don't think you can get away with giving me rubbish like that!' I snapped at him, thrusting the decaying dictionary back into his hands. 'Give me a proper one right now!' He took a step back. For a moment he looked at me. By now my eyes were blazing with anger and my hands were trembling. He glanced away and handed me a whole dictionary. 'No need to make such a fuss about it,' he muttered as he walked away. That was the first and the last bullying I had at Chew Valley School.

    I loved lessons, especially English. Mrs Long had encouraged us to write imaginative descriptions and now I had the chance. History fascinated me, especially Elizabeth I. Starting at secondary school, I shed both weight and wheeziness and even began to enjoy games lessons. The exception to this was gymnastics. This was the era of Olga Korbut and Ludmilla Tourischeva. Skipping ropes and ball games were set aside at lunchtime. All the girls wanted to be gymnasts and spent every spare moment practising flips along the paved walkways. Spectacular sequences were achieved as an everyday event. Taking a short run-up, girls from my class would flip over up to three times in a row. Such enthusiasm was exploited by the P.E. staff, who made giving a gymnastics performance in pairs a routine part of our lessons. This was sheer joy to most of my class. However, for Claire and myself this was not good news and we paired up together out of necessity. Our best and, especially in my case, virtually only achievement was the ability to do an ordinary forward roll. Backward rolls were harder to control. To show willing, we also threw in a cartwheel as part of the routine. Sadly, my feet never

A new friend

got more than a few inches off the ground, though Claire was a bit better. Armed with these moves, we had the challenge of making up a five minute sequenced gymnastic display to perform to the rest of the class. Our forward rolls were interspersed with as much creative prancing and coordinated arm waving as possible. Then, as a dramatic climax, we attempted a cartwheel leading into a final forward roll, finally straightening up to a Y-position, with feet together and arms stretched out over our heads.

Gradually, Claire and I became good friends. I realised that this had happened one day on the coach when Jane turned around to talk to me about Guides. 'We've been thinking and we wondered if you'd like to come along to Guides with us. It's at Bishop Sutton, so you'd have to catch the 6.15 bus at the end of your road. We'd already be on the bus so we could show you where to go. Guides doesn't start until seven o'clock, so we always go and see our Grandma for a bit. You can come too. Grandma says she'd like that. If you want to, you can come along tomorrow. You'll just need your bus fare plus 50p for subs and wear a blue skirt and jumper if you can. It doesn't have to be that but as near as possible would be good and you won't feel so out of place.'

The following evening, needless to say, I stood on the grassy verge at the edge of the road, clutching a selection of coins for the bus fare in one hand and a torch in the other. There were no street lights and I was forty yards from the nearest house, so most of the time I was

Along Featherbed Lane

enveloped in darkness with only the small circle of light on the ground from my torch to keep me company. Every few minutes a car would come round the bend with its lights blazing at full beam, making me turn my head away. I had to listen carefully for the sound of an approaching bus. Eventually, I heard a sound approaching that was different from that of the cars that had hurtled past, something slower with a rattly hum from its engine. I stepped to the edge of the verge as the bus turned the corner and held out my arm. Sure enough, it ground to a halt just past me and from seats near the middle of the bus I could see Claire and Jane waving at me.

Now that the journey had begun, the evening, like the inside of the bus, was bathed in soft, golden light. First stop was their grandma's house. We were welcomed in out of the cold, dark night into a room with a coal fire crackling away merrily. Then, as a special treat, we were offered a tin of wrapped barley sugar or butterscotch sweets to choose from. I was made very comfortable, treated with great kindness and no fuss. Claire and Jane just had time to tell their grandma how the rest of the family were keeping and which instrument grades they were working for this term. Before we left, their grandma held the school jumper sleeve that she was knitting up against Claire's arm to check the length. Then we hastily slipped our coats back on, loath to leave this haven sooner than we needed to. 'Bye, Grandma,' Jane said, gently manoeuvring us towards the door. 'Must get these two going or we'll be late!'

A new friend

Going to Guides became a highlight of each week. I was enlisted as a member of Claire's Kingfisher patrol. Our Guider, Mrs Atcherley, was a kind, cheerful, well-spoken lady, who truly cared about us girls having the opportunity to 'make the most of ourselves'. She generously allowed us to have camps in her grounds. These were times of great fun and companionship for me. Before the actual camp we spent an evening at her home, learning skills with tents and campfires. Instead of our uniform, we were told to wear trousers and jumpers.

To Dad's horror, I now had several pairs of trousers owing to the strict instructions of our Guider, who insisted that we wear them for hiking and camping. Mum had longed for a little girl 'to dress up' and I was normally happy to oblige, enjoying the prettiness of cotton frocks in summer and colourful skirts and jumpers when the weather turned cold. However, an order was an order. Still, I placated my Dad by wearing a very pretty mid-blue jumper that his Auntie Nem had recently passed on to me. It was made of cashmere and was the softest, snuggliest garment that I had ever worn. It was worth folding my arms just to cuddle the sleeves.

After several hours of struggling with heavy wooden poles and bewildering yards of canvas, we were allowed the treat of going to meet our Guider's pet goats. One nanny was particularly affectionate to me, nuzzling up to my hand for endless strokes and tickles behind the ear. 'Come along, girls,' our Guider gently chided us. 'You really should be washing your hands by now and

Along Featherbed Lane

finding your coats. Your parents have already started to arrive.' I got ready as quickly as I could, scrabbling in the pile of coats to find my anorak so as not to keep Claire's dad waiting. During the journey home, we practised our campfire songs. 'Kookaburra sits in the old gum tree', 'Kalinka' and 'Ging Gang Goolie' echoed around the car, with Jane putting in an alto line.

Soon we were back at Bromley and I was hastily saying my goodbyes and thank yous. I burst through the shop door, clutching my kit list and permission form. I couldn't wait to tell Mum and Dad all about my wonderful evening. I hung up my anorak in the hall and went through to the living room where Mum and Dad were cosily settled down for the evening, watching the television. As always when I'm excited, I waved my arms around as I started to explain what the campsite was like. I was amazed at the horrified expressions that came over their faces.

'Christine, dear,' Mum began, 'what on earth has happened to your beautiful jumper? I can assure you that it wasn't like that when you set out this evening. Ted, it's the one that Auntie Nem sent her just this Monday. I can't believe that it's ruined already but just look at that sleeve.' Following their gaze, I looked down at my right sleeve but, seeing nothing unexpected, I twisted my wrist around. I couldn't believe my eyes. There was an enormous hole gaping most of the way between the cuff and my elbow, several inches across.

A new friend

'Chrissie,' Mum said more gently, with a coaxing tone, 'whatever happened? If someone was bullying you, you can tell us. You do know that, don't you?'

'Of course I'd tell you if there had been a problem', I mumbled, 'but I just don't understand what's been going on. It's been a lovely evening and nothing horrible happened, honestly!' Realising that we were getting nowhere, Mum made me a hot chocolate and then sat down to hear the tale of the evening. It was as I reached the end and mentioned the loveable goat that she suddenly started laughing.

'That goat wasn't being affectionate, she was just eating your jumper!' At first I didn't believe her but Mum and Dad eventually convinced me that goats will eat absolutely anything. It was certainly the only explanation that made any sense. I went to bed scandalised by the sheer cheek of that goat.

The next morning I remembered to hand the camp forms to Mum.

'Well I never,' she exclaimed loudly, 'I'm certainly not having this. There is no way on earth that I am giving permission for you to go mountaineering. And as for potholing, the very thought of it makes me shudder. I don't care what the other mums agree to, no child of mine is going to be exposed to such danger.'

No amount of pointing out that our camp was going to be in the grounds of our Guider's house, with the only trip being a short hike around a few local fields, would calm Mum down. In the end, she only signed

Along Featherbed Lane

the form having emphatically crossed through both mountaineering and pot-holing. As for the kit list, Dad got quite excited at the prospect of lending me his Second World War bedroll and kitbag, not to mention the monsoon cape. I began to feel a bit less excited at the thought of this camp.

'I can't believe how many clothes they're asking you to take just for a weekend,' Mum reflected. 'Mind you, I suppose we need to make some allowance for food rations for the goat!'

Chapter 16: Camping

My days at camp were mercifully free of mountains, potholes and hungry goats. Instead, they were filled with aching limbs and an endless supply of new tasks to learn, or at least attempt to learn, cheerfully. However, the fun of being surrounded by friendly people of my own age both day and night was more than enough compensation.

Pitching camp was the first challenge. As Patrol Leader, Claire chose a couple of us to help collect our tent. By the time that we got to the front of the queue, several of the others were already laying out their ridge tents on the grass and checking where each pole slotted. However, before handing over our canvas, the Guider took a long, straight look at Claire.

'Well, Claire, as one of the more experienced patrol leaders, I'm giving you the bell tent.'

Something flickered across Claire's face but whether it was disdain or delight was too hard to tell. The bell tent was a sturdy structure, which radiated out from a central pole. It looked older and shabbier than the ridge tents but somehow that felt quite in keeping with my camping gear. With the monsoon cape spread underneath as a groundsheet, my Second World War bedroll was a massive affair of khaki canvas held together with brown leather belts and slightly rusting buckles. My backpack was matching issue, canvas supported by a heavy iron frame and held together with leather straps. Dad's obvious delight that his old kit was going to serve a turn

Along Featherbed Lane

again needed to be brought to mind as I glanced enviously at the lightweight royal blue nylon bedrolls and cushioned camping mats of the other girls. Still, in the musty khaki there was a permanence and a link with home which I appreciated.

Thankfully, there was little time to be homesick, as there was a constant round of chores to keep the camp running. We took it in turns to help with all the different jobs. The main challenge was that of keeping us all fed. Some fetched kindling and larger pieces of wood for the fire, some carried water to the campsite, whilst others helped to prepare and cook the food. At the beginning of the camp the pans were coated with a thick paste of washing powder mixed with water, which was allowed to harden off as a protective layer to shield the metal pans from the worst effects of the flames. After all the extra exercise and hours of fresh air, the food tasted wonderful. My favourite, though, was apple crumble, with the crumble topping cleverly made of crumbled-up digestive biscuits. After this we tidied and washed up, using water heated over the fire. By then we were very tired and only too glad to gather round the campfire to sing songs. The tune of 'Kalinka' still danced through my head as I tumbled into my sleeping bag.

It was strange to wake up to see the domed canvas roof of the tent above my head, with the sunlight pricking its way through the dense fabric. There was precious little time to lay there, though. Claire was already sitting bolt upright in her sleeping bag. 'Time to get up, you lot,' she

Camping

called to us. When there was virtually no movement from any of us she continued, 'You've got to get a move on, otherwise you won't have time for a wash.' The thought of a nice, hot, perfumed bubble bath trespassed into my mind. Then I remembered. I had helped to put up the wash cubicles the previous afternoon. They were as tiny as the canvas cubicles that housed the chemical toilets. How were we going to get clean in there?

    The answer soon came as we stood in a queue and were each handed a small, round plastic bowl. Reminded that all the water was precious, as it had to be carried by hand to the campsite, we were given a couple of inches of cold water with a dash of hot water from the kettle, which had been simmering on the campfire. Armed with our bowl balanced between both hands, our towel and flannel dangled over an arm each, our half a bar of soap clutched precariously in the hooked fingers below one side of the bowl and a plastic mug with a little clean, cold water in for cleaning our teeth plus our toothbrush and paste in the other hand, we waited our turn for the wash tent. When at last my turn came, I flapped the canvas door aside and found myself alone in the dark, dank space. In front of me was the only bathroom furniture, three strong sticks tied together above half way and fanned out to form a tripod on which to balance my bowl of water. Remembering the length of the queue behind me was enough of an incentive to make sure that this was just a lick and a promise of a wash.

Along Featherbed Lane

Soon the daily round of fetching and carrying wood and water, tidying tents and adjusting guy ropes was underway. By early afternoon, we had finished washing up from lunch and had gathered enough supplies for making tea later on. 'Right, girls,' our Guider announced, 'go and have a rest in your tents. Make sure that you have a proper rest. In this heat you must take enough rest and drink enough water or you will start to feel very poorly indeed and we don't want that now, do we? After your siesta, I've planned something a bit different for you to do.'

It was good to be away from the searing sun, laying on our backs, allowing the heaviness to seep away from our flopped-out arms and legs. As we fell into quietness, I could hear the background drone of bees and crickets still bustling about their chores.

When at last we heard a call of 'Come along, girls, that's enough rest for now,' we emerged blinking into the sunshine. 'You're going to need a sun hat on this afternoon and I don't want to hear any excuses. Sun cream would be a good idea as well. Let me know if you forgot to pack any and I'll see what I can do.' We all bundled back into our tents and reappeared a few minutes later, our arms and faces smeared with white streaks and a range of floppy blue hats on our heads. Within a few minutes we were sorted into twos and threes to go tracking. Jane and two more of the older guides were sent ahead with a good time allowance to lay the trail for the rest of us to follow. I was very pleased to have been put

Camping

with Claire, as I had great confidence in her guiding ability and I looked forward to being able to have a chat as we went along.

It wasn't long before our team was allowed to set off. As we clambered over the first stile, Claire explained that we would have to keep a very careful lookout for twigs and stones. I must have looked a bit dim, as Claire went on to explain the art of girl-guide tracking, which used nothing but easily available natural materials to provide the signs. A sign was needed at every possible convergence of tracks, either to confirm the old route or to divert you over a gate or along the side of a different field. Having read the sign ourselves, it was then our duty to make sure it was still neatly placed and easy to find for the following team. Whilst all went smoothly, this was great fun and we found our directions easily at every point and hurried on as fast as possible in the hope of catching up to those who were ahead of us.

Sometimes clues were less obvious and the sun beat down on us as we scoured the cracked earth for possible combinations of twigs and stones. Finally, we saw a promising-looking stile across the field. As we drew near we spotted a huddle of ladybirds perched on it. Sure enough, in the dusty approach there was a distinct arrow of sticks leading us over it and on across the field towards another obvious gate. After that the trail sped easily across fields decked in scabious and knapweed. Even the hot, humid air was aflutter with Red Admiral and Cabbage White butterflies. As the final arrow led us

Along Featherbed Lane

back, we emerged triumphantly back at the campsite and made for our tent for some rest in the shade before the next round of chores. Inside the tent, the heat was still sticky and unpleasant. After a fairly short break, we were called out to make a start on tea.

'Come along, girls, let's do our best to get tea ready before the weather breaks. Once we've eaten we can shelter in our tents and it won't matter if the rain falls.'

We all scampered around fetching and carrying, trying not to get in each other's way. It was good to sit down at last with a plate of blackened sausages, mashed potatoes and peas on our laps. Sure enough, thick black clouds were invading the summer sky overhead, giving the light a sickly yellow tinge. We ate, drank and washed up as quickly as possible. Just as we were tidying away the plates, large drops of rain started plopping around us.
'Into your tents now, girls,' our Guider called out. 'We'll have to forget the campfire for tonight but you may sing amongst yourselves if you wish. Patrol leaders, please check on your guy ropes and make sure that the pegs are in properly and that everything is fastened down. Don't leave anything outside your tent and do it quickly before you get soaked!'

It was a rather bedraggled Claire who joined us safely in the bell tent a few minutes later. As she opened the door flap, lightning forked across the sky behind her, chased almost immediately by a deep volley of thunder. Protected by nothing but a frail layer of canvas, we felt

Camping

the ferocity of the storm. 'Move all your stuff away from the edge of the tent and, whatever you do, don't touch the canvas or it'll start leaking!' Claire shouted at us between the thunderclaps. Fumbling for our torches, we followed her advice. Just as we were beginning to feel a bit more snug and secure, despite the storm raging around us, the tent started to creak as a strong gust of wind buffeted the canvas like a sail and tussled with the guy ropes. 'Everyone in the middle!' Claire yelled at us. 'Hold onto the central pole to stop it from falling.'

From the nearby tents there were screams and shouts as the wind managed to claw a fingerhold under the edge of the ridge tents and tossed the canvas up into the savage air. The Guides inside tried to catch hold of the wildly flapping tents but all too soon the poles, which had been dragged this way and that by the wind, collapsed in a heap. Peeping out from the flap of our tent, we could see a line of refugee Guides clutching bedding and backpacks, making their way through the storm to our Guider's house on the other side of the orchard. I gave a little shudder as I wondered how long it would be before our tent crashed to the ground. 'Don't worry,' Claire muttered, 'this old tent has no intention of falling down. If there's one thing that a bell tent is good for, it's staying put in a storm.'

For a few moments I glanced enviously across at the house, which was snuggled down in a dip between the trees. Golden light was pouring through the gaps in the curtains and even mellowing the curtains themselves with

Along Featherbed Lane

a golden richness. It would have been good to escape from the spitefulness of thunder and lightning, wind and rain. Then Claire closed the flap and our eyes needed to adjust to the torch-lit dimness of the tent once again. With a sigh, I realised that it was good to have been given the bell tent. Hanging onto the central pole brought the four of us closer together: Joanna, with her shoulder-length red hair framing her pale face, Rosalind, anxiously flicking her long fair bunch over her shoulder and Claire, tense and tired with responsibility but still trying to look after us as she had been taught to do. 'Right, then,' she chipped in between the claps of thunder. 'I think it's about time for a song. Let's start with "Kookaburra" and then take it in turns to choose, going round clockwise.' So it was that we waited out the storm, singing ourselves hoarse over the howling wind, until all was peaceful and, exhausted, we let our weary arms drop and fell asleep.

Not all camps featured storms, just most of them. One particularly enjoyable one was held at Yeo Valley Farm, a local dairy farm which had started to branch into yogurt production. We were to travel there by bus, as the camp was over the weekend and, to make the most of the time, we were to start soon after school on Friday. Quickly changing into my jeans, blue jumper and blouse, I managed to get up to the main road at the agreed time to get on the same bus as Jane and Claire. Breathing heavily as I pulled my kit up the steps of the bus, I eventually reached the driver. I'd done it.

Camping

'Where'd you wanna be going, my luvver?'

Turning scarlet, I realised that I had no idea. We must have been told at some stage where the farm was but I hadn't been paying attention. Hunching forward in the hope of disappearing a little from view, I turned to look along the bus. Never had I been so glad to see my friends waving cheerfully at me.

'Excuse me a moment, I've just got to check,' I mumbled. By then, however, Jane and Claire were chorusing, 'You want Blagdon.'

Embarrassment soon gave way to wonder as we were taken out of the familiar reaches of the Chew Valley along the high, winding road through West Harptree, past the pond in Compton Martin, past the signs to Ubley and down the steep hill towards Blagdon. This was more dramatic scenery than I was used to. Here the Mendip Hills towered above whilst the patchwork of lush green fields tumbled gently down into the still blue of Blagdon Lake. I was very excited that the farm was so close that it too dipped its toes in the lake. Our camping ground was within easy walking distance of the farmhouse, to which a small posse of guides was sent periodically to fetch canisters of water. Our field was vibrant green, rippling with wild flowers and butterflies and with a panoramic view over the lake that made us feel small and awed. Normally our presence turned our Guider's paddock into a campsite. Here, though, we were tented like mushrooms on the landscape, just here for a short while.

Chapter 17: High days and holidays

When we moved to Bromley, family holidays became a thing of the past. I have some happy memories of going on holidays to Harris's farm and also of staying at 'Uncle' Dudley's country guest house, with its fascinating model village and train track in the garden. To Mum's frustration, these were a little truncated, stretching from Sunday to Friday, as Dad was determined not to miss out on a Saturday's trading. Nevertheless, they were wonderful times of freedom and fresh air, of petting the Harris family's Border collie, of being in awe of the enormous cows as they fretted and kicked out a little on their way to the milking shed and of being enchanted as I clambered among the toy-sized houses and farms loving made by 'Uncle' Dudley. At Bromley, Mum fulfilled her long-awaited ambition to live in a village, which had been previously placated with countryside holidays. In any case, within a short space of time, Dad's poor health would have made holidays impossible for him.

It was my brothers and sisters-in-law, with their families, who ensured that I still had the pleasure of holidays. Judith's parents Harry and Sadie lived in London and very kindly invited me to stay with them so that I could see the sights. The Tower of London, Whipsnade Zoo, Buckingham Palace and the Science Museum dazzled me but what I enjoyed even more was playing with their Border terrier Timmy and helping to take him for walks on Wandsworth Common. I was made

High days and holidays

to feel very much at home. Although I was used to picking berries from hedgerow and garden, Sadie introduced me to one I had never encountered: the loganberry, which she made into delicious pies.

Laura's family also kindly included me in their family holiday to South Wales. The journey itself was an adventure, as Patrick, Laura, her little sister Sarah and I went in Patrick's Ford 'Pop'. I loved this aged black box of a car for its airy height, which did not provoke my usual carsickness. We travelled at a leisurely pace, apart from when gravity assisted us on long steep downhill sections of the route, when the speedometer wavered up to 50 mph amid loud cheers from us! I remember driving in horror past the vast, belching chimneys of Neath and Port Talbot and arriving with great relief at the small seaside resort of Ferryside. Once inside the cottage they had rented, there was immediate concern that none of the kitchen utensils promised in the listed equipment were available. It was only after some time of general outrage that we noticed a small latch on a wood-panelled wall and realised that this was the door to a cupboard under the stairs. Once opened, this proved to be an Aladdin's cave of aluminium pans and colanders, graters and sieves. The holiday could begin.

Although I had spent many days out at Weston-super-Mare, this was a very different and exciting sort of seaside. The waves were so close and powerful. Rather than building sandcastles, our time was spent playing in the water, floating on lilos, allowing the incoming waves

Along Featherbed Lane

to toss us closer to shore. Then, in the stillness of sunset, Laura would teach us how to skim small flat stones across the surface of the water. Chasing the pathway of molten sunshine across the darkening sea, our stones bounced happily away, sinking only to be washed clean back onto the beach for the following morning.

A university friend of Jonathan's and his wife owned a holiday cottage in the Cotswolds and I was invited along to share in some lovely holidays there. Picking our way along the edge of a huge field of wheat, following a right of way was a new experience for me. When I still lived in Bristol, my brothers used to take me to the huge green expanse of Downs to play French cricket and football. Countryside at Bromley meant mostly walking along Featherbed Lane, gathering wild flowers. Exploring the fields for mushrooms meant risking being chased by cattle, who always seemed to be hidden from view in some distant corner of the field until you ventured far from the gate. The knowledge that there were official footpaths through some fields was a revelation.

If we needed to fetch provisions from the village, Jonathan would take me along by car, freewheeling down Bredon Hill as far as possible. My favourite day trip from there was the Cotswolds Farm Park, with its amazing traditional breeds of farm animals. In the evenings, it was fun to snuggle up and play card games in the little cottage. We were not the only ones to think so. One evening we noticed that a family of tiny field mice had

High days and holidays

joined us. Squatting on their haunches with their front paws propped up on the edge of the carpet, they were making sure that they had a good view of these strange people who had invaded their privacy.

A few years later I set off for another holiday with Laura's family, this time to board a plane to visit Patrick and Laura, who had emigrated to Canada. I could hardly wait to see them again and I was glad to be spending more time with Laura's family—Reginald, Julie, Jeffrey and Sarah—, whose kindness and good humour had helped to make our stay at Ferryside so much fun. To my amazement, all of us fitted quite comfortably into Patrick and Laura's car, which had a vast back seat and room for an extra front passenger.

Patrick and Laura's condominium was in a block with its own swimming pool and table-tennis tables and seemed to me the height of luxury. Added to this were wonderful day trips. Watching the sheer heft of water passing us from the Scenic Tunnels behind Niagara Falls, taking the glass-sided lift up the side of the CN Tower, weaving our way through the wilderness of Algonquin Park, all these and many more were extraordinary, breathtaking experiences. There were also quieter days, which were lovely too. Paddling a canoe on Little Doe Lake and visiting the Black Creek Pioneer Village offered more time for reflection and chat. As a special treat one evening near the end of our holiday, we had plate-sized steaks at Ed's Warehouse, followed by a helpful stroll to Laura Secord's for maple and walnut ice cream. All too

Along Featherbed Lane

soon the holiday was over. I dreaded having to say goodbye, not knowing how long it would be until I would see Patrick and Laura again and wishing that I could put my feelings into words. I returned home with my thick mop of hair having been beautifully styled at Vidal Sassoon's in Toronto, an extremely generous gift from Patrick and Laura, who had worked so hard to give us all the most wonderful holiday possible.

Mum especially was entranced and longed to hear every detail of the trip. Whereas Dad had been to America, Ceylon (Sri Lanka) and Burma (Myanmar) as part of his service during the Second World War, Mum's furthest trip abroad was to Wales and she felt short-changed. She was particularly sad that she had never flown.

Still, Mum, Dad and I were soon treated to a visit from Ghana by Jonathan and Judith with their baby daughter Rebecca. I was used to baby kittens but nothing had prepared me for how adorable Rebecca was or for her tiny fingers that would reach out and encircle one of mine. Two years later they also brought with them their beautiful new baby Emma, who was the daintiest little person I had ever met, with large blue eyes and blonde curls.

Primary colours tumbled across the faded shades of home, as we sat on one of Dad's home-made rugs and played with the red and blue Tupperware shape sorter ball, helping Rebecca and Emma to slot the different shapes into the right holes and then spilling them out

High days and holidays

again over the rug. My brother Jonathan had been transformed into a father, wearing a brightly coloured loose Ghanaian shirt embroidered with intricate patterns of joromi, with Rebecca or later Emma carried on his back or perched on his hip. It suited him. Judith had very kindly made dresses for Mum and me and had them decorated beautifully with traditional swirling patterns of embroidery. Mum's was a blue and white paisley dress and mine a plum colour, with a band of golden embroidery across the chest. Such a richness of colour transported me away from my everyday surroundings.

During their stay we had a day trip to Weston-super-Mare. Passing a sign offering light aircraft flights over the bay, Jonathan joked, 'There you go Mum, it's your big chance. Would you like to go flying after all?' Jonathan carried on driving. Mum, however, said in a clear and decisive tone, 'I don't know why we're still going. You've just offered me a flight and my answer is yes.'

A short while afterwards, somewhat to the amazement of us all, Jonathan, Rebecca, Mum and I were being swooped over the beach and soaring up and away over the rising land. A little turbulence was added when Rebecca, who was sitting on Jonathan's lap, playfully caught hold of the joystick. Mum was delighted and happy to be assured that this trip provided a greater sensation of flight than being on a transatlantic flight.

It was apt that Jonathan provided this flight of fancy for Mum. Whenever possible, as far back as I could

Along Featherbed Lane

remember, he would visit home for Bonfire Night, armed with a generous box of fireworks. Catherine wheels, fountains and rockets lit up our faces, crackling through the chill autumnal sky. With woollen-mittened hands, we wafted glowing patterns with our sparklers in the darkening air.

Chapter 18: Jennie

Family birthdays passed by pleasantly but without undue fuss. As a young teenager, I remember once being allowed to ask two friends, Claire and Rebecca, round for a birthday tea. Before tea we were allowed to spend an hour or so in my room, munching Turkish Delight and listening to a cassette of the Beatles. Since my handheld player also had a microphone, we played around recording ourselves singing and chatting and listening back over the recording with a mingled sense of pride and embarrassment. How could that rather affected and squeaky speaking voice be mine?

Eventually Mum called us down to tea: a choice of sandwiches and a bag of crisps each, followed by a homemade birthday cake covered with white icing and decorated with tiny chocolate drops and glacé cherries. As an extra treat, there were also slices of chocolate biscuit cake. I loved helping Mum make this, putting Rich Tea biscuits in a bag and then smashing them around with a heavy wooden rolling pin until they had been crushed into crumbs. These were mixed with melted margarine, raisins and cocoa powder and pressed into a well-greased baking tray. When this had cooled down completely, often after a spell in the fridge, Mum would melt squares of cooking chocolate and pour the flow of molten chocolate over the biscuit base and allow that to cool down before scoring it into squares.

Along Featherbed Lane

After tea Claire and Rebecca politely thanked Mum. Claire even mentioned that she was really glad that Mum had chosen glacé cherries to decorate the cake, as these were her favourite. Mum's eyes twinkled with pleasure at this useful titbit of information. Throughout our years at Chew Valley School, Claire and I remained friends and I don't think she ever visited us without Mum offering her some sort of home-made cake topped with a cherry.

I loved visiting Claire's home. Claire lived with her mum, dad, two sisters and brother in a cottage in the middle of a field. Claire's mum gave such a kind and warm welcome that I felt completely at home. Whilst we worked away at one end of the long dining-room table on homework projects or Guide badges, she would be ironing at the other end of the table. 'You girls never run out of things to talk about, do you? I'd love to be able to chatter away like you do. I certainly love hearing you.' Music would be floating across the corridor from the living room where the other children were taking it in turns to practise for their latest music grades.

I remember being invited to Claire's older sister Jane's birthday tea, just two days before my own birthday. Dainty triangle sandwiches were piled high and, most excitingly, there were little cooked and cooled sausages. Jane's cake was brought in with the candles lit and her cheeks glowed and her glasses sparkled with the reflected light as she blew them out. Just then, their Mum disappeared once again into the kitchen and came back

Jennie

with another cake, also decorated with Smarties and silver balls. 'Now, Christine, since you can't have egg you wouldn't be able to enjoy Jane's cake with us, so I've made you a little cake for yourself. You can have a piece now and then take the rest home for your own birthday.' I was speechless with delight. Even without candles, my eyes shone and my face was flushed with excitement.

My birthday was exactly one week before Christmas. Sometimes this meant that I was on holiday; sometimes it was the end of term. This year, for my fourteenth birthday, it was the very last day of term. After a long assembly with the house points cup being awarded, we had a normal timetable, though not even the teachers were in the mood for study.

Just before lunch we had maths with our rather quiet, serious and elderly gentleman teacher. I was always very much in awe of Mr Bentley and tried to remain as invisible as possible in his classes, with my head down whenever an answer was requested. Unlike many of our teachers, he was not to be distracted in idle chatter but calmly and resolutely taught us mathematics and nothing else. It was a pleasant surprise to us all that he announced that we were going to spend the lesson doing maths puzzles and tricks. To my amusement, he started by asking us to think of our date of birth. Claire glanced sideways in my direction and gave me a quick smile. Then, after a series of additions, subtractions, multiplications and divisions, we came up with a number from which he offered to tell us when our birthday was.

Along Featherbed Lane

First he asked Christopher, then Pat. 'Just one more,' he muttered, scanning the classroom. It must have surprised him that for once I was not studying my textbook or my knees but looking up at him eagerly. 'Christine, what number did you end up with?' he asked kindly. Once I had told him a smile started to curl the edge of his mouth before he restrained it. Instead of telling me the answer, he just started singing 'Happy Birthday' to me, to the astonishment of the class.

We were allowed home after lunch, which was an especially useful treat as we always decorated the Christmas tree on my birthday. I spent the afternoon fixing the tree into a sturdy pot inside a burnished metal wastepaper bin in the corner of the front room. Many of the decorations were post-war silvery metal, some with a dash of white or pale pink paint and some silver baubles. There were a few folded paper decorations that had been made during my time in Mrs Long's class and carefully stored away each year. There was also a lovely Father Christmas on his present-laden sleigh and a collection of seashell shapes in different pastel shades of tinted hard plastic, which gently spun on their threads and shimmered in the sparkle of fairy lights.

Mum, Dad and I ate a contented birthday tea in the glow of the tree. For once no customers interrupted the meal and we enjoyed sharing the lovely cake made by Claire's mum and basking in the kindness of it. 'You must remember to send our thanks again when you see Claire tonight' Mum reminded me several times.

Jennie

Tonight was very special. This year the school disco had fallen on my birthday. Although I felt too shy and awkward to enjoy the dancing, I always enjoyed the chance to dress up and spend time with my friends. I had new clothes for my birthday that I had chosen from Mum's catalogue. With bright purple flared trousers, a long-sleeved ivory blouse with sleeves which puffed in the lower arm and a collar that looked like Fred Basset's ears, along with a knitted top with half-length sleeves in purple, yellow and orange vertical stripes, I was the height of fashion for once. Mum had even wound up my hair with strips of rags for an hour or so before I left so that my thick mop of brown hair had some bouncy curl to it.

The evening passed far too quickly. Softly lit with coloured lights, the school hall was transformed. The hall itself was set several steps down so that it seemed to fill with rainbow colours, music and dancers, like a lake of wonders. The higher level at the side of the hall, where the teachers sat at assembly time and along which we queued for lunch, became a dazzling gallery from which to enjoy the spectacle below.

All too soon the lights dimmed for the final dance and then the normal, cold fluorescent hall lights were switched on, making us blink back into reality. The hall was just a place for eating school dinners again, with a worn, wooden floor and frayed curtains that didn't quite meet. Still, it had been a lovely evening to end a very

Along Featherbed Lane

happy birthday. I was glad to be going home, snuggled down in the corner of Claire's dad's car.

When I arrived home, much later than usual, the shop was in darkness. To my surprise, however, both Mum and Dad hurried into the shop to meet me, looking very twinkly eyed and excited. Mum started talking straight away.

'Chrissie, dear, you know the clothes and books we gave you this morning? They weren't your only presents from us. There is one more, special surprise that had to wait until now. We have been ringing around for days now trying to find one for you. Then this very afternoon someone said to try the Stoke Inn. I rang the lady and she was ever so pleasant and said that yes, they did have just one left and we could have it if we could collect it. I explained that we don't have a car but that maybe we could get a taxi. She said she'd see what she could do this evening when the customers were in. Anyway, she asked the regulars and several of them said they knew Bromley Stores. Fancy that, all the way over in Chew Stoke. Anyway, one of them was just finishing his pint, so he said he'd pop it in to us on his way home. Of course, this meant that we didn't have a chance to see it first but I still think you'll like her. We think she's sweet, even if she isn't a great beauty. I'm sure she's got plenty of character.'

Mum had meanwhile been leading the way slowly, oh so slowly through from the shop into the living room. 'Chrissie, what do you think?' she whispered, pointing to

Jennie

a little round ball of tortoiseshell fur curled cosily in front of the glowing embers of the fire. I was down on my knees in a moment, hardly daring to breathe. As I sank onto the rug beside the kitten, it stirred and stretched its tiny paws towards me, opening its eyes sleepily. I had never seen a cat like it before. Her face was divided into quadrants of different colours: black, brown, ginger and white. With a little white bib and paws, she was dainty and utterly loveable.

We soon discovered that the new kitten, who I named Jennie, was unusually beguiling. A measure of her charm was that she quickly won the heart of our now elderly matron of a cat Tiggy. Jennie had a sweetness about her that was irresistible. She made the most of this with adorable poses. Somehow, she had learnt to beg and did so with great daintiness whenever she needed anything. If she wanted to gain your admiration, Jennie had perfected the salute, balancing on her haunches and flicking her right paw over her ear. It wasn't only for the benefit of the family that Jennie performed her tricks. She had favourite customers who she listened out for. As soon as she heard their voice, she would prance into the shop and balance elegantly on the top of the gate that separated the well of the shop from our serving area. From this prominent position, she performed a spectacular sequence of begs and salutes before stretching her neck forward for a tickle behind the ears from her admirers. This proved to be almost too successful. One customer became so besotted with Jennie that he offered a substantial amount

Along Featherbed Lane

of money for her and became quite angry with Dad when he pointed out that, as my much-loved pet, she was definitely not for sale.

    A time was coming when we would all leave Bromley Stores but for now this was still home and it was Christmas Eve. My calico kitten Jennie was the most wonderful birthday present I could possibly have had. No Christmas present could possibly match her. Still, I put out my pillowcase as usual, wondering what the morning would bring. The bitterly cold room and my excitement made it hard to fall asleep. Morning came at last, with icy fingers, and bright white light filtered through the deep frost inside the window. My filled pillowcase had been placed near me, so that I spotted it as I opened my eyes. On the top was perched a fairly small parcel with the label 'Happy Christmas, darling. Hope you enjoy this until it's time to get up.' This was a long-standing tradition. When I was little there would be a doll for me to play with until Mum and Dad woke up at seven o'clock. This looked more like a book. That was fine. I snuggled down under the bedclothes and started reading. Going downstairs half an hour later, I perched on the end of my parents' bed clutching my pillowcase and also the bag of presents I had bought them from Woolworths on my last visit to the dentist in Keynsham: rose-scented talc, a 4711 cologne stick and Crème de menthe Turkish Delight for Mum and Old Spice pre-shave and aftershave and a box of Assam tea for Dad.

Jennie

Gathering up plates, cups, knives and forks, we made our way through to the living room for breakfast. The curtains were drawn and the room was hushed in shade. The Christmas tree glittered dimly in its corner. As we came into the room something stirred in the tree's branches. As we watched in amazement, we saw that a wren had taken shelter there from the cold night. It cocked its head and peeped at us warily. Then, gently as thistledown, it flew off and headed back along the hall to the shop, where it circled until Dad opened the door and it soared back into the brightness of morning.

www.ingramcontent.com/pod-product-compliance
Lightning Source LLC
Chambersburg PA
CBHW030040100526
44590CB00011B/279